❖

My Friends the Senses

❖

❖

❖

❖

Père Boulogne is the author of a number of books, of which MY FRIENDS THE SENSES is the first to be translated into English.

My Friends the Senses

CHARLES-DAMIAN BOULOGNE
Dominican

TRANSLATED BY
JANE HOWES

FOREWORD BY GERALD VANN, O.P.

P. J. KENEDY & SONS · NEW YORK

MY FRIENDS THE SENSES

is a translation of *Mes amis les sens* (Paris, La Colombe,
1951).

BF
233
B642

LIBRARY OF CONGRESS CATALOG NUMBER: 53-11511

Copyright 1953 by P. J. Kenedy & Sons, New York

PRINTED IN THE UNITED STATES OF AMERICA

Foreword

THE SORT of world in which most of us have to live today can make it very hard for us to be truly and deeply natural, very hard not to lose our roots in Nature altogether. Cooped up in our vast amorphous modern cities, remote from the realities of Nature, from field and forest and green growing things, from the rhythm of the seasons; occupied with work that may well be either purely cerebral or purely automatic; surrounded by the sort of commercialized sex which can make even love in the end unnatural because depersonalized; surrounded also by the sort of climate of opinion which views the scientific-rational approach to reality as the only one of any great value or validity—it is hardly surprising in these circumstances if we become cut off from our roots. And yet, when a thing is cut off from its roots it must inevitably wither and die. A society that becomes progressively more and more remote from its natural setting must of necessity become more and more sick, neurotic, etiolated. That is the measure of the importance of Père Boulogne's book.

If you treat education, for instance, as a matter simply of imparting information to the young, information about matters of fact and above all of scientific fact; if you leave the whole of their intuitive life, their sense-perception of the beautiful and their emotional reactions to what the senses reveal, to look after themselves; rather, if you stifle all this by cramming their heads with knowledge of the purely factual, utilitarian, commercial, you send them out into the world with truncated personalities: you make it more or less impossible for them to live life fully and deeply and richly; you may help them to be masters of the surface-knowledge of things, you will not help them to "listen to the essences of things."

And many of us are in fact in this plight. We see things, we do not stop to look at them; we hear but do not listen. The business of living must go on, we say, and we have no time for these refinements. . . . But in fact it is the substance we are missing. Having eyes we see not and having ears we hear not. "Our vision," writes Père Boulogne, "too often lacks breadth, depth, and particularly the objectivity that it should have. Our attention is limited to the things we need. As for other things, we scarcely glance at them. . . . We are ignorant of nearly all the treasures sight would give us." So it is also with the other senses.

Guardini writes in similar vein of how, with the birth of the modern world, man "lost his living contact with real things" and became the man of "the towns, of ideologies, of formulas"; no longer rooted in "the profound order of life," the "natural rhythms of day and night, of the seasons . . . [he] could no longer perceive the message of things . . . he could only see them now in the light of brute matter, as objects of pursuit and possession, of commerce or research." [1]

That is why we have to re-learn what we have forgotten,

[1] *Esprit de la Liturgie*, p. 66.

have to learn again like little children to look and to listen, learn with eyes and ears and hands, learn afresh the earth and its fullness, learn again those intimations of immortality which come to us from the heart of things. The senses are our friends, if only we can make them an organic element in a unified personality. They are more than that: they are the indispensable channels through which we arrive at a deep knowledge of reality. Just as love-making, in which all the senses are engaged, is robbed of its glory and meaning if it is treated simply as a pleasurable activity instead of as a way in which two people gain a profound knowledge—a *connaissance cordiale*—of each other; so with all the other uses of the senses: you must look, not merely see; you must listen, not merely hear, for only so will you come in the end to the living essences of things.

How are we to learn these things? I have attempted to answer that question at length elsewhere, in a book which at many points touches on the theme of this volume.[1] For the purposes of this foreword I can perhaps do no better than quote here, as I quoted there, a passage from Evelyn Underhill's *Mysticism* in which she shows us how we may teach ourselves awareness, teach ourselves how to achieve "a real communion between the seer and the seen." All that we are to do, she tells us (remembering, however, that "it is a practical experiment on which we are set; not an opportunity of pretty and pantheistic mediation"), is to take "some simple, concrete, and external thing"—an acorn, a leaf, a "hazel nut," some small living thing, and then to look at it, but really to look. "Wilfully yet tranquilly refuse the messages which countless other aspects

[1] *The Water and the Fire*, Collins, 1953.

of the world are sending; . . . concentrate your whole attention on this one act of loving sight. . . . Do not think, but as it were pour out your personality towards it: let your soul be in your eyes. Almost at once, this new method of perception will reveal unsuspected qualities in the external world. First, you will perceive about you a strange and deepening quietness; a slowing down of our feverish mental time. Next, you will become aware of a heightened significance, an intensified existence in the thing at which you look. As you, with all your consciousness, lean out towards it, an answering current will meet yours. It seems as though the barrier between its life and your own, between subject and object, had melted away. You are merged with it, in an act of true communion: and you *know* the secret of its being deeply and unforgettably, yet in a way you can never hope to express." [1]

And as we can learn to look, and so really to see, to know, with the eyes, so also with the other senses; so that music, for instance, ceases to be for us a vague background noise and becomes a communication, a communion; and the sense of touch becomes a means not just of sensuous or sensual pleasure but of deep understanding and love of things.

For indeed this is not a question of an esthetic expertise, in the way a developed sense of taste provides the gourmet with his pleasures. It is a question primarily of becoming liberated from our isolation, our loneliness, and becoming again rooted in nature, in the universe, in all being. It is more than that. For if we have learned to be natural contemplatives, merged with reality in an act of true com-

---

[1] *Mysticism*, pp. 301-2.

munion, we may find it easier to become contemplatives
in the greater and deeper and supremely important sense:
rooted not merely in nature but in God, aware not only
of the earth and its fullness but of eternity, filled with the
life-bringing love not merely of finite things but of Infinity.

And being much more alive ourselves, living much more
richly and deeply, we shall have that much more to offer
to God, that much more with which to praise him. The
"Canticle of the Sun" will be for us no strange echo from
an unknown and alien world but a song of our own hearts;
the *Benedicite* not something we let the Church sing for
us but a song in which we are ourselves identified with the
Church and with the universe in whose name it sings.

To those who think of the Church as ruthlessly Mani-
chean, an enemy of the flesh and of the senses, this book
must surely come as a salutary revelation. To all of us it
can bring the help we need, to put to better use the gifts
that God has given us to worship Him with, and to make
our lives as a whole a better offering, a richer song of praise,
than they would otherwise be.

GERALD VANN, O.P.

Contents

❖

Introduction

OF ALL the tools we can use, the one we could not do without, the closest one to us, is the body. It is also, alas! the least understood. Even many people who are experts in mechanics are ignorant of the workings and the possibilities of the body that companions us in all our doings.

And yet the work the body does for each one of us is more important than the work of any lifeless machine can possibly be. There is nothing in us which has not entered through the gateway of the senses, and which the senses have not transformed into living sensation. The senses introduce us to everything, provide us with everything.

Let us leave to scholars and moralists the sad work of underlining and emphasizing their drawbacks; the Church accepts and respects the senses. Knowing the place they occupy and the primal part they play in the development of personal life, the Church wants us to be their friends.

But all friendship should be clear-cut and lucid. That is why I have written these little studies of a few of our chief sensory contacts. Technicalities here play less part than a concern to put into relief the inestimable value of the living capital at each man's disposal, the value of the treasures which no force in the world can keep us from acquiring freely. For the Lord has so made us that, come what may, the largest part of our inward growth remains primarily dependent on the use we make of these gifts we have received.

Note: The reader must not expect to find here a study of the moral problems concerning sensibility. Without entirely excluding them, the present study bears especially upon the human and religious values of certain principal manifestations of sensory activity.

C.-D. BOULOGNE

First Part

❖

GRASPING FROM AFAR

❖

❖

❖

❖

CHAPTER I

Looking and Seeing

> If you love a flower that lives on a
> star, it is lovely to look at the sky at
> night. All the stars are blossoming.
> —Saint-Exupéry, *The Little Prince*.

1.

THE SENSE OF SIGHT is so important in our lives that
we usually do not think of its sensual side. Even casual
references to its physiology and to the acts proper to it are
spontaneously understood as symbols of spiritual activity.
Popular language furnishes us with many examples of this
strange twisting of words, examples that are really tributes
to the sense of sight. Sight is so important to us that when
we wish to judge or express or suggest the importance of
something, we can find nothing better with which to compare it. Sight is our instinctive measuring-rod.

Vision and life are so closely linked together that one phrase is enough to sum up the terrible wrenching achieved by death: "He has closed his eyes."

Carnal beings that we are, we get out of our depth in the invisible world, even though the highest part of our nature entitles us to admission to it. We hurry back to our images, which, sadly enough, are imperfect. The images that are the least deceptive, because they best suggest our highest actions, are those that liken them to vision. Thought, knowledge, art, intuition, and contemplation are all compared to vision; and we call the mind "the eye of the soul."

Such expressions as, "He sees rightly," "He sees everything," refer as often to quality of judgment as to the keenness of bodily eyes. "He can't see a thing" refers less to myopia of the physical organs than to spiritual myopia, a shortsightedness that ranges from thoughtlessness to stupidity.

The way we value our eyes serves also to measure our feelings. To cherish someone as "the apple of our eye" expresses the highest tenderness; "I can't see him at all" expresses the deepest antipathy. To say, "When we deal with him, we must keep our eyes open," means that we do not trust him; and to say, "We can keep our eyes shut with him" shows confidence in him. And to say, "I have lost sight of him" expresses the whole desolation of a friendship made barren by separation.

The phrase "to see someone" expresses the best part of all our encounters with people. Without the discoveries we can make by actually seeing a person, how superficial our relationships would remain; and how could we ever decipher the secret of faces, capture their smiles, count their tears? These silent messages would never be received! What other means of knowing shows us anyone as clearly as sight does? The way the eyes take possession is as total and overwhelming as any action can be. Nothing about the cherished being can escape them; subtly and unsparingly they drink it in and devour it.

And they read a person at a glance, in his features, but more than in any other way in his eyes. In his eyes we read the last word of the enigma. In and through their brightness, their color, their beauty or banality, shines another light and lives another flame which, as well we know, does not come from the daylight reflected there, but from the silent fires within. We know, by instinct, that the relationship between these two living crystals and the most secret part of a man's soul is so close that it synchronizes them even in their most subtle movements.

It is hard for eyes to deceive. Their play is so terribly spontaneous that it is harder to guard than that of the lips or the hands. It is more difficult to discipline our glances than our faces. Even the man who has the greatest mastery of himself rarely succeeds in putting anyone off the trail in this way. Sincerity, calmness, nobility, and depth do not live in the eyes unless they already dwell in the heart.

The incredible swiftness of the eyes allows them to speak a language that makes the language of the lips take second place where feelings are concerned. In love, silence is worth more than language; and the eyes have the best of it there. The lover seeks the glance of the cherished one, and draws a response from it, food for love.

> When toward thee all my desires depart in caravan
> Thine eyes are the wells where all my weariness drinks.

From the eyes, not from the too-clever lips, we learn whether we are really loved, appreciated, understood. From them, for our happiness or unhappiness, we draw our sharpest certitudes in this important realm. We are at the mercy of a glance. What do words and gestures mean, if the eyes belie them? If the eyes show indifference to us, the visible presence can be compared only to a body without a soul. When "the heart is not in it," the ties are cut, and people discover that they are strangers, farther apart than the stars at the opposite poles of our immense universe.

> I am less far from the secrets of the other world than from the secret of those eyes

Golaud sings sadly to Mélisande, who has once again retreated into her inaccessible solitude because of her hopeless love.

Poets or not, it is from the eyes that we receive the most precious of our treasures: sweetness and joy, understanding and encouragement. And through them also we suffer, no less surely, the sharpest pains: ingratitude, disdain, criticism, and discouragement. But there is nothing in the world we value so highly and dread so much as being able to see.[1]

---

[1] Let us notice in passing how much the importance of sight has emphasized the urgency and seriousness of certain principles of practical conduct. "To keep one's eyes open" sums up the counsels of prudence. "To learn to see clearly" shows

Since we value sight so highly, how is it that we take so little care how we use it? In most cases we are very far from getting from our eyes the most that they can do for us.

Our vision too often lacks breadth, depth, and particularly the objectivity that it should have. Our attention is limited to the things we need. As for other things, we scarcely glance at them. So we pass by so many people, so many faces and scenes, without noticing them at all. We are ignorant of nearly all the treasures sight would give us.

This visual negligence, regrettable in itself, has dangerous and dreadful results. If we have only a confused sight of things, we misunderstand their originality and their worth. How can we do justice to things we have observed so carelessly? If a man never sees things straight, he runs a grave risk of depending upon only a priori ideas and prejudices to which reality hardly ever corresponds. This is why most of our judgments are gratuitous and unjust.

The richness and rightness of our spiritual vision depend largely upon the keenness and careful use of our eyes.

If an activity is easy for us, we tend to be less careful about its use. Seeing is facile and quick, and so we tend to think we have seen perfectly at first glance. We have an

---

the sad benefit of bitter experiences. "Blind trust" costs dearly! If we wish to avoid becoming victims of illusion, error, and the lies of tricksters and cheats, events and circumstances force us to "look out." The only information we can fully depend on is what we have acquired—and verified—for ourselves. "To keep watch," "to keep our eyes open" is, here and in every domain, an indispensable precaution.

(*Translator's note:* The author's point is emphasized by the fact that these expressions and idioms based on seeing are found also in English.)

impression that all we have to do is open our eyes in order to see the world. Do we see it well, for all that?

Our too-brief glance grasps nothing but a confused image, a vague reconstruction of the whole object. The only thing deserving the name of vision is that which perceives and retains the whole and all the details of complex realities. In order to obtain this, the quickest and most practiced eye cannot disdain the conditions imposed by its structure.

Because it is a living organ, the visual apparatus has a mode of registering different from photographic instruments, whose functions are purely mechanical and chemical. Its sensitivity to light, form, and color, far from being purely passive, requires an assimilative reaction. The eye sees the realities from which light waves are brought to it only in the measure with which it transforms them into nerve impulses from which the brain in its turn shapes images to feed the memory.

This prodigious work, which the eye accomplishes automatically under the impact of light, is not instantaneous. It takes a certain amount of time for the organism to accommodate itself to the strength of the light and the conditions of distance at which the object is presented. The eye must focus properly on the object. When this adaptation is made (and how many times a day it takes place!) the eye is able to exercise its proper activity—that is, of penetrating and detailing the divers elements of the reality it is observing.

❖

The secret of visual attention does not lie in ready-made formulas. It is not a question of seeing a great deal or of seeing very quickly. It is a question of seeing well, or of seeing better. The art of looking at things presupposes a discipline, whose first law consists in accepting a relative slowness. The eye is nothing like a camera, whose speed can be quickened at will. It is a living organ; it imposes its own rhythm, denoted by a certain patience. The best observers always take their time.

But if we are to devote more time to the consideration of realities than our laziness and a pure utilitarianism would suggest—for these are content to notice only what is enough for their absolute needs—we must be inspired by a higher motive. Only the heart and the mind are capable of claiming a meticulous and penetrating application from the eyes. To linger in the observation of things other than the self implies a profound conviction of their worth.

Most people, it is true, are interested only in things that are somewhat showy, bordering on the banal. The importance of reality eludes them. A curiosity that only the extraordinary and the novel can awaken is very indolent. So-called good taste, which is capable of appreciating only great efforts, usurps its name.

By comparison the works of very great artists, painters, or sculptors seem to proceed from more down-to-earth minds. Most of them, in fact, devote themselves to realities that are very ordinary and often commonplace. The subjects of the greatest masterpieces are taken from elements and scenes in which, if left to themselves, many superficial minds would never have seen any beauty. Many works of this sort teach us what is hidden under appearances, things we never suspected! So before a crowd of faces and of scenes we find ourselves adapting the celebrated jest of the man to whom the paintings of the Master had revealed the poetry of the countryside: "Haven't you noticed how often lately nature has been imitating Corot?"

2.

This concern to find the beautiful through and within the least of things does not come from a dilettantism in reverse. More or less consciously, true artists obey a sort of instinct of orientation which urges them to find positive beauty, not in systems or abstractions, but in reality, in whatever form it exists. The solidity and firmness of concrete beings represent a value whose very certainty guarantees the presence in them of this other more subtle and secret wealth that we call beauty.

The beautiful is not necessarily the dazzling and noble thing we too often believe it to be. It is, surely, "that which is pleasing to the sight," as St. Thomas had it; but the admiration it arouses is not necessarily immediate. To reserve the name of beauty exclusively for things that awaken enthusiasm at first glance is equivalent to making each man's personal taste the sole criterion of worth. Our spontaneous acceptances and rejections depend upon the immediate agreement of what we see with our predilections, our habits, our mentality, and our education. Since these are all necessarily limited, they are incapable of opening to us any aspects of beauty with which they are not already in tune.

But beauty, a deep-seated property of being, transcends our categories. Its conditions were never submitted to our

arbitrary definitions, our codifications, our preferences, or
our habits. In every way the riches of the world surpass our
ideas and our vision. Our very first duty is to recognize this
fact and adapt ourselves to it. Not without humor, Chesterton has defended the right of artists to respect the originality of reality by regarding it through their own eyes and not
through any "canons" whatever:

> In the name of beauty, the Greeks have deceived and
> tyrannized over humanity. All of the marvelous works
> they have made for civilization should not conceal from
> us their great and terrible sin against the variety of life.
> Nature wanted each face to be as individual and as
> expressive as possible, so that we could distinguish it from
> all others as easily as we distinguish a poplar from an oak
> or an apple-tree from a willow. But the Greeks have
> treated the human form as Dutch gardeners treat their
> trees: they have lopped off its living limbs to give it a
> shape which is academically conventional. With the im-
> passivity of a gardener, they have pruned the nose,
> trimmed the chin, and have succeeded in making us find
> ugly the faces which are the most powerful and the most
> lovable, and in making us find beautiful the faces which
> are silliest and most inexpressive.

With all due deference to current opinion, brilliance of
color alone and grace of line alone do not make beauty.
The pleasure and admiration that beauty evokes rise from
causes which are less loud, more subtle—causes dwelling
on the same level as the essential texture of reality. The
secret of beauty is identified with harmony and order, with
exact balance and fair division of the different elements

that make up a being. In this profound coherence rests both the existence and the truth of each being.

What do appearances matter here? The fact that they are dazzling or discreet, rare or commonplace, complex or very simple, constitutes only the superficial aspect of beauty. Beauty is something infinitely more precious: it is the fundamental harmony that assures the stability of a being, and so posits it as an irreplaceable unity and a reality not to be equated, under this form and according to this modality, with anything that resembles it. If it is not beautiful with this essential beauty, no other being can be, and no appearance, opulent or poor, can have existence. Far from corresponding to a standard type, true beauty is as varied and as original, as fanciful and as unexpected as each thing that exists, for each thing is in some way unique.

Without having any explicit knowledge, every authentic artist has an instinctive certainty of this truth. Hence his infinite respect for even the smallest details.

"The point in question," said Fromentin in his *Maîtres d'autrefois,*

> is to become humble for humble things, small for small things, subtle for subtle things; to gather them all up, without omitting or disdaining any, to enter familiarly into intimacy with them, to enter affectionately into their manner of being. This is the work of attentive curiosity and patience. Therefore genius consists of guessing at nothing, of not knowing what we do not know, of letting ourselves be taken by surprise by our model, asking of a thing only how it wants you to picture it.

To this respect for the nature of a being the artist must add an immense patience. Many realities do not yield their

secret at the first attack. Inexplicable caprice and uncon-
strained whim seem to have presided over their making,
dealing out shapes and traits, patterns and sizes, colors and
shadows. But this apparent chaos is only superficial; a mysterious order—and that is exactly what we must discover—
dominates and justifies these contrasts. Somewhere in this
being, harmony must exist; for if within these elements incoherence is absolute and contradiction is total, the individual could not exist at all.

Where is the center of equilibrium, the focal point, at
which diversity is unified and the wavering lines form into
order? "Beyond the lines that we see," said Leonardo da
Vinci. It is to discover this that the artist is ever striving.
The secret of beauty, mingling with the secret of being,
lives at the heart of reality.

In this search, whose aim is like that of the scholar and
the analyst, the artist proceeds according to his own methods. His eyes are the unique instruments his instinct for
beauty uses. They alone can document it; he puts his trust
in them. That is why his very first care is to make an ally
and a guide of the thing in which all vision must exist:
Light.

Seen in exactly the right light, every being seems less
commonplace. Excited by this discovery, the artist then
undertakes to penetrate into the mystery. Suddenly his
observation ceases to be passive. His eyes then become like
the instruments that allow observers of the night to search
into the details of a suspected field.

This labor of analysis is slow and austere. It must go be-

yond the joyful but rather superficial warmth of spontaneous admiration. It must take possession, in an orderly and
precise manner, of an individual or a general effect. First,
to recognize its elements, line by line, design by design,
color by color. Then to grasp the place and weight, role and
quality of each one—in brief, what the language of the
painter calls value.

To this dissection, which is the only thing that can
lead us further into the understanding of beings, the greatest artists have consecrated intensive labor. Innumerable
sketches bear witness to the minuteness with which they
have studied their subject. This is a far different thing from
the ordinary opinion, which sees in works of genius the
happy result of a mysterious fever or an inspired frenzy.

"Before color comes design," say the masters. That means
that before the composition there must be examination,
and then the clear, wise, attentive, faithful transcription
of the hollows and high places of the texture on which the
shapes depend and the colors play.

Let us not deceive ourselves, however. Such analysis does
not have for its sole purpose the making of a true copy of
observed things. For the artist it is the means of discovering
the secret of beauty which mere appearances could never
yield. Having grasped it, it is this beauty above all which he
intends to emphasize with the means and style at his command. And in his work, sculptured or painted, we find
reality again, but a reality translated and interpreted; not
simply repeated, not transformed or deformed, but explained and clarified, because he has read and deciphered it

from within, as his heart has understood it. As for us, because we are busy people or bad observers who have not known or been able to understand these things, the work of the artist enables us to see the harmony lying hidden in each thing which constitutes its beauty, and also the relations and harmonies that make up the charm of the general effect. It is as if they were remade before our eyes, as if the artist figures out and repeats the great alchemy of creation upon a less elaborate design. So let us listen to the strange but enlightening words of Cézanne: "I bow before the intelligence of the Father Almighty."

The artist's attempts to explain reality have followed different roads and have used different methods and procedures. People who do not know the difficulties posed by the very complexity of truth are astonished at this. But how could human genius be able to drain the content of even the smallest bit of reality into one work alone? Art, like all abstract thought, cannot pretend to translate the concrete adequately. All created representations, intellectual or artistic, must necessarily remain partial. Why should we ask of painters and sculptors what nobody would ever dream of demanding from scholars and philosophers? To re-create anything with true adequacy would be to wield the infinite power of the original Author, the power of the Creator Himself!

Interpretations of beauty only translate it, and each after his own manner. Some insist on color, some on shape; some on light, and others on perspective. All have at heart the purpose of telling what they see as they see it. Above all, they try to make us see it a little as they have seen and loved it.

These efforts have led to the rise of many schools and have occasioned many disputes. Let us try, however, to admire the deep and sincere love of truth which all these works imply. Fromentin has warned us:

> Just as there are in life most practical motives that elevate our way of acting, so also in this art, which is said to be so matter-of-fact, in these painters who are called mostly shortsighted copyists, you feel a height, a loftiness, a goodness of soul, a tenderness for the truth, an enthusiasm for reality, which give their works a value that the subjects do not seem to have. Hence their ideal, an ideal somewhat misunderstood, somewhat disdained, but indubitable for one who wishes to grasp it and very attractive for one who knows how to savor it. Sometimes a warmer grain of feeling makes them thinkers, even poets.

3.

The art of observing, so necessary for appreciating the beautiful, is no less essential for attaining truth. In gaining wisdom, eyes play the first part. Without them we could not follow an experiment in the laboratory.

The gifted inventor owes his most wonderful discoveries to his applied, concentrated vision. Have we taken enough notice of the visual humility at the source of the most sensational discoveries? While most people reserve their attention for grandiose spectacles—the only ones worthy of interest, in their opinion—the noblest minds have been bent over ridiculous bits of reality. An apple or a cheese, rats or dogs, seeds or microbes are treated by them as impressive mysteries. In these things, which the masses think are insignificant, geniuses have discovered the most profound laws of nature and of life, of physics, and of chemistry.

Even if most of these men remain unknown, their example has inspired modern scientific disciplines. Are the most advanced techniques, in their methods and instrumentation, anything more than a perfection of the art of looking at things? Whether it concerns things extremely great or extremely small, observation conditions all progress.

As profoundly as painting, science in its own way teaches us that the sense of sight is the primary tool of the mind for grasping the richness of the truths among which we live. Whether it is a question of discovering or controlling, the information that our eyes bring makes the laws, and there is no appeal from its findings.

We admire the results of all these works, artistic and scientific, but the secret of their genesis eludes us. Since we are indifferent about trying to plumb the depths, we often attribute these results to the happy coincidence of exceptional gifts and miraculous luck. This facile explanation dispenses us from drawing from facts the lessons they contain.

In most successes, personal effort plays the chief part. The most penetrating and fruitful observations are more deliberate than spontaneous. When all is said, the final secret of a man's output is, most of all, a function of the love that animates it. If artists and scholars are not passionately in love with beauty and truth, how can they wear themselves out with such work as they exact of their eyes?

Contrary to the popular proverb, love is not at all blind. Only the one who loves beings for themselves looks at them with perfectly clear eyes. The attention he brings to them knows nothing of the veils and prisms that intercept and distort egotistical views. For a basely acquisitive heart, the only important viewpoint is that of financial interest and values.

The discovery of the true secret of things presupposes a disinterested viewpoint that can proceed only by the way of love. Only a truly loving heart is generous enough to accept things for themselves, with all their differences and their worth, even if they disconcert and dominate him. What heart, if it truly wished this objectivity, could not gain it? Even if a man is not an artist at all, he can look at the beings surrounding him, not in criticism or judgment, cupidity or jealousy, curious vulgarity or a partisan prejudice, but as a friend. To see them and to discover that they are at one and the same time similar and original. Different, no doubt, but, like himself, living, tested and tried, sorrowful and afflicted.

To observe men with the eyes of the heart makes us literally discover what they are. Whoever looks at them with the best of himself finds a thousand reasons to cleave to them. Theirs were the faces of which Bernanos said, "Dear faces, which have seen good and evil, have braved life and death." Each man carries some poignant story engraved in his heart. Jacques Rivière was right in saying, "Now we know how to be happy, simply for this reason: In the crowd we have meditated upon a face which perhaps was not beautiful." Simply because it was the face of a man, the face of a brother.

Seen in a daylight undarkened by selfishness, even inanimate realities would seem quite different. We should rediscover them, all of them. Actually, we see them so little, so badly. Anxieties and avid passions are so many blinders that limit our sight. There are so many speeches about those fools of painters and poets who give their lives to something that does not sell! People do not suspect that, if they do not nourish themselves with these realities into which the Lord has put freshness and light, human eyes will soon wither and decay. The stars and the fountains, the dawns and the light, the days and the nights, the forests and the seas, were given to us so that, when we looked at them, our eyes, however tired they might be, would become peaceful and clear, and so that if we lacked anything better, we should know in this world here below at least a minimum of purity, truth, and peace. In his own way, in his admirable book *The Little Prince*, Saint-Exupéry has taken up the eternal theme of the Canticle of Canticles:

> "People had stars, but they were not the same. For some, who are travelers, stars are guides. For others, they are nothing but little lights. For some, who are scholars, they are problems. For my businessman, they are gold. But all those stars are silent. You—you alone—will have stars like no one else."
>
> "What do you mean?"
>
> "When you look at the heavens and the night, because I am living on one of them, because I am laughing on one of them, it will seem to you as if all the stars are laughing. You—only you—will have stars that know how to laugh!"

Finally, we cannot forget to point out the important work of the eyes in that subtle contact with another mind which is reading.

First of all, the grasping of sense from signs is surely a mental work. The office of the eyes is purely material. But the way we understand a passage depends so much on the behavior of the eyes that it is important to consider it.

Many of us must admit that our progress in this field often goes backward. Habit has made us the victim of the two demons, quantity and haste. Reading much, we read badly. Rare are the times when we receive and retain a deep impression of what we have read. This evidently results in part from the lack of substance in many writings, but it is due even more to our lack of application. We treat books as we do everything else: we cast a glance at them, perhaps, but certainly we do not look at them carefully enough to fathom them.

Quick as it may be, the mind's grasp presupposes the grasp of the lines by the eyes—and this takes a certain minimum of time. The physiological rhythm of the eyes cannot by hastened at will. When we are reading, visual assimilation is slower. Even though we are used to written signs and to the vocabulary of a language, reading confronts us with unproved combinations where each detail can be extremely important. If reading is to remain objective, to deliver the goods of a book completely, it must be, if not meticulous, at least exact. So we see how important it is to discipline the eyes; this is a condition of enriching the reader's mind from the author's mind, a key to that astonishing and disturbing miracle which makes us the beneficiaries of the most valuable works of human thought across the barriers of time and space.

We owe to our eyes the biggest and best part of our wealth. Every object of our thoughts and feelings has passed through their double door. They are the tireless purveyors and faithful interpreters of our inner life. Whether we give or receive, our eyes take part. They are both the creditors and the debtors of the mind and the heart. Their structure, all physical as it is, does not keep them from acting as faithful servants of the mind.

❖

CHAPTER II

Revealing Light

God said, "Let there be light!" and
there was light. And God saw that
the light was good.—*Genesis*.

1.

LIGHT is one of the very few things in this world which
has escaped both distortion and criticism. Everyone feels,
more or less confusedly, indebted to it; and, however pro-
saic he may be, he, like St. Augustine, hails it as "my eyes'
best friend."

Light consoles the sick, soothes the uneasy, delights the
artist, stimulates the worker, encourages the unhappy. Lazy
and wicked men dread the daylight but do not dare to
slander it. Any man would think it the greatest misfortune
to be deprived of light.

It is offered freely to all, but this marvelous treasure loses
none of its integral richness in the sharing. Of all our bless-
ings here on earth, this is the only one whose distribution
awakens no jealousy. As St. Thomas finely remarks, it has

succeeded in being at one and the same time the most delectable, the most coveted, and the least disturbing.

Radiating everywhere and falling on everything, light knows nothing of wear and tear. It seems unchanging and eternal. Nothing that it touches destroys it. This is one of God's gifts which He gives liberally and conserves jealously. He has made it the visible image of both His perfect purity and His unapproachable transcendence. Human genius can discover its laws and imitate it, but we cannot regulate the unfolding of the day itself. Nothing with life or feeling may approach its flaming source, under pain of death; millions of miles of distance, myriads of degrees of heat forbid us ever to approach it.

It does not at all astonish us that the ancients gave divine honors to this fiery star! Poor, dazzled men, in this way they honored the real cause of the most beautiful gift from on high. Without God's special revelation, man would never have been able by his own power to free himself from the enchantment of the sun's radiant splendor. So the first thing that the Bible took care to explain was that light was one of the inanimate creatures. Dazzling though it may be, its perfection does not approach the perfection of man, its debtor. When Revelation had made this fundamental point, it added precise details that do not in the least belittle light. Its splendor is the reflection of another, entirely immaterial splendor. To our minds, so little familiar with the invisible, the glory of the daylight serves to introduce us to a greater glory. It lets us foresee—or, to be more exact, helps us to imagine—the marvels of a world whose incommensurable beauty far surpasses the beauty of the morning and the evening which delight the eye of man.

Through daylight also we learn the value of the spiritual and moral perfection of which it is the chosen Biblical symbol. Christ conferred a supreme dignity upon it when He claimed it as a personal attribute: "I am the Light of the world." When He wished to show us more plainly the importance of His mission to our minds and hearts, He compared it to the part the sun plays in the universe.

Thus we know that Revelation does not belittle the importance of light, but sanctions and amplifies it. The serious lessons centered on this symbol inspire us to examine more carefully the source of light itself.

There are two means of doing this, very different in their method and language—scientific analysis and direct examination.

The technical studies that scholars elaborate require a special preparation. The very style of their formulas and the way they express their results run a grave risk of disappointing those who are seeking especially to understand better why light attracts them so. Light seems to them to be very clear, plain, and friendly. But when the geniuses of modern physics talk about it, they translate it into difficult formulas and they give analyses of it which are matters of opinion rather than absolute certainty. This is a far cry from the artless impressions of those whose chief wish is to explain to themselves why they love light so much. Scientific formulas can tell them nothing about it; the thinking of pure scientists is a sealed book to the layman.

But should they reject science, for all that? No, it does not seem that they should. Perhaps if they would try to put their confused impressions into a little better order, they would gain in knowledge; not a strict scientific knowledge, but a better awareness and a more joyful appreciation of the miracle their eyes behold every day.

The appearance of the light is for us the appearance of the world. Revealing reality, light allows us to perceive it. The night blots things out, confusing them in a nameless mass; light restores them again and shows them in their own original complexity. The sun rises; and without sound or shock, the world emerges and settles itself, becoming mountains and valleys, trees and fields, houses and streets. Even the imponderable is identified. The noises of the night lose their confusion and show their origins. We can identify them—the murmuring of water, the sighing of the wind, the rustling of leaves, the echoes of human footsteps. Individually and together they have meaning from the moment light makes them clear to us. We owe to light the ability to distinguish them, to appreciate and recognize lines and values, patterns, masses, compositions, and perspectives.

Only with daybreak begins plain and sure perception, clear consciousness of presences, exact knowledge, and controlled estimates. In spite of the certainty of its existence and the stability of its structure, reality, without the light that shows it to us, would remain forever something to be guessed about, guesses we could never verify. This most fragile and most imponderable of all realities conditions the discovery of the importance of other realities.

What is more delicate, more subtle than light? Its power

is universal and cannot be denied. Light forms and molds shapes, distinguishes and determines volumes, wakens and brightens colors. This is so true that the ancients gave an exquisite definition of these last: *"Color est lux incarnata,"* "Color is light incarnate." The physicist would find fault with this definition but the painter and the maker of stained glass delight in it. Without color, how could they hope to woo something so elusive as light? We can evoke and suggest it only through its fugitive incarnations: the brightness of tints and the play of colors.

Alas, no brush could ever catch the most precious and living thing, its very mobility! Even if sometimes they might be able to capture a momentary brightness, great masters of painting must never hope to render the infinite series of gradations through which light passes insensibly, without breaks or clashes. Only the living eye, thanks to its wonderful power of accommodation, has the power to follow the continuity and variety of this untiring play of light. And every one of these changing colors reveals many deep truths to us.

Color does not merely show us reality, it gives a value to it. So we come to respect and admire it. Far from harming what it touches, light gives importance to it, ennobles it. Without it, how commonplace many things would seem, how chaotic many groupings would appear! So, enlightened, we at last understand the words of Scripture: "God saw all the things that He had made, and they were very good."

What seems to be more free than the course of the sun? The sun does not think of poverty or opulence, or of the depths or shallows of the things on which it shines. An inanimate star, it passes by, as remote as it is indifferent. Yet an ineffable justice and mercy are exercised through its soulless action. Nothing is forgotten or neglected. Its diffusion allows it to work the entire field of the visible world, and its variations reveal the diversity of all things. The world is not made up of identical beings. All have their own faces, demanding a unique lighting. Each hour of the day, each degree of light, has its more favored and less favored ones. But light is so rich—and the Power that presides over its distribution is so tender—that there is no reality, however humble, which does not find its moment of grace when the light blesses it and reveals its beauty.

To this providential and free gift—which no one would know how to hasten or prolong—the ephemeral creature owes its moment of glory, its fleeting triumph. And this precarious tenure of light intensifies the emotion and the value of these merciful moments, these brief instants when, through His light, God seems to smile on them just enough to allow us to discover the very real beauty of these material realities which, otherwise, would be nothing but motives for profit or for suffering. One chance is offered us to see them with other eyes than those of greed, care, or grief; to reconcile us to them and, seeing them for themselves, to give them full justice.

More than books, light teaches us wonder. It offers to the poor and the unlettered marvels which they can understand and with which they can feed their souls. And it does this without any limitation, for, unlike the schools of men, the school of light can never be monotonous.

Illumined by ever-moving brilliance, the spectacle of the visible world varies from moment to moment, taking on a vivacity that makes us see all its secret richness. Under its delicate sovereignty, everything is lighted and animated. Landscapes come to life, mountains move, rivers gleam, the sea glistens. Mass loses its heaviness, motionless things their fixity, the permanent loses its monotony. From morning to evening, from summer to spring, over the inanimate universe the day pours out light that is never frozen, never the same. Lighted by it, identity loses its rigidity.

Whoever follows the untiring movement of light can never again see the world as inert, as if all were petrified, congealed, final. The quickening touch of light almost allows us to catch a little glimpse of the very joyousness of being. Through the enchanting renewal of tints and shades, contrasts and harmonies, shines the all-powerful process that conditions and harmonizes the whole of creation.

The Bible teaches us that God created light first. Our hearts understand this instinctively. Light must have welcomed and bathed a world born of unthinkable Purity. By its brilliance, extending over all things, created eyes could see the splendor of the Source. So, at the same time, there were imposed upon man the value of existing things and the transcendence of Him to whom he owes everything. Among so many enigmas and mysteries, complexities and cares, light brings us its message of wisdom. It is so beautiful that in spite of our troubles and doubts we can see nothing in it but the subtle signature of God.

To describe the action of light we must think of the most delicate and noble causes. Our conception of power involves a modification of something inferior: to act is, for us, equivalent to making or changing, imposing our ideas upon a being different from us. It gains, perhaps, by the act (at least in our eyes) but it loses its native originality. Our victories depend upon the defeats of others. But light is something new and different, for its action requires neither sacrifice nor victim. It is pure benevolence, a gift without compensation or return.

Light does not modify, alter, or use things. Sometimes we call it violent, overwhelming, wounding, or harsh. We are unjust; we blame it for the weakness of our own eyes. Really, its contact is infinitely more gentle than that of the most exquisite touch. Under its weight, even the most slender leaf was never bent, or the tenderest blade of grass, nor the most fragile thread of the Virgin. The touch of light has never tarnished the bloom of a petal nor bruised the down of a butterfly's wing. More intangible and swifter than the winds, but without their unforeseeable and dangerous caprices; its course, from dizzy heights, is as regular and calm as faith.

Can we muse upon its benefits without thinking of those of the Divine action itself? It does not overpower the world, over which it has passed tirelessly throughout the thousands of millenniums. All it does is communicate to it its inexhaustible freshness and its imperishable novelty. It is indeed the servant—and the answer—of the creating Spirit, of whom it is written that He renews and preserves the face of the earth.

The earth, the old earth of such remote beginnings, immensely weary, so long used and worn, is daily renewed and reclothed in a mantle of light, each day as new and as beautiful as on the morning of that day when the Lord willed it into existence. The world spins and circles, circles and spins and turns inexorably, and wears out; the light never stops shining. But the light remains the same. Neither time nor change has any power over it. It alone escapes alteration. In the heart of the universe, ruled by change and its pitiless demands, the light of the day, so marvelously unchanging, recalls to us the existence of an indefectible duration. It is the sign, if not the proof, that even here below all things are not so ephemeral as our disappointing experiences would lead us to believe.

Its appearance alone, so fresh, so new, keeps us from giving in to our fear of change and loss. Each morning the daylight teaches us that, in spite of our growing old and spent, the source of all light and of all beauty continues to exist, to shine, and to act. Why should we give in to useless repinings? Losses and destructions are the inevitable price of ever-changing duration, but they have no effect on the best of things. Beneath all changes and alterations being remains, and its existence and value are at least as important as those of the light that visits it.

And the day is the moment of hopes and plans that would be inconceivable were we not profoundly optimistic of the final result of our efforts. But would this fundamental feeling exist if the light did not, by its very appearance, help us to overcome the sadness and scandal of the ravages of time?

This is not its only benefit. A terrible temptation lies in wait for our insatiable hearts: it is boredom. Its causes are multiple and, in their different ways, unavoidable. One, and not the least, is the monotony of too-familiar surroundings. Accustomed to one environment, our attention ceases to see it, and looks out on emptiness; and soon we experience a sickening madness that invades our thoughts and feelings. We can no longer endure such a place, yet, at the same time, our work keeps us there. Therefore we feel a need, which soon becomes unhealthy, of distracting ourselves, of changing—and that as quickly as possible. Stability, however indispensable to real productivity, becomes impossible. The breath of attention becomes shorter and shorter. A sort of spiritual asthma takes possession of our consciousness and energy. This "suffocation" soon paralyzes and sterilizes our whole life.

Distractions remedy this condition, as do changes of scene. But they remain very precarious if one is not in addition very susceptible to light.

Its very variations make it an immensely resourceful magician, a conjuror of spectacles astonishingly diverting, because so varied. Light variegates and blends in countless ways the hours and the seasons. But, above all, it has the strange power of making us look at the most familiar surroundings with eyes that are ever new. While it modifies the coloration of things, it also affects our state of mind. The pure and serene joy of dawn passes into our hearts. The exaltation of full day stimulates us. The serenity of evening lulls us. We are elated by the light of the springtime, ex-

alted by the light of the summer. The sweetness of autumn
mellows us, and the melancholy of winter saddens us. We
can never find the world always the same.

So light preserves us, in a large part, from the tedium that
monotony invariably engenders. Indefinable as it is in itself,
its power of revelation cannot be questioned. Examples are
far from rare which prove that it is the light of a familiar
landscape that awakens and satisfies the curiosity of the
most ravenous observers in the world—the painters.

It is sad that so many human beings do not know how to
get their share of these enriching and sobering lessons. The
spectacles that the silent light at every moment offers and
renews for everyone are never advertized with a great splash,
and so they do not attract those unsubtle people whose
attention requires a fanfare of publicity to awaken it.

But to these also light offers its benefits. Its munificence
is not contingent upon praise or gratitude. Obtuseness, in-
comprehension, or rejection do not lessen or injure it. It is
too great to implore or beg. Its action does not depend
upon those on whom it falls. It is sufficient unto itself. It
comes and goes, with kingly freedom in its opulence. In its
magnificence it remains the same. Hence its equal liberality
to all.

Thus, in His Gospel, Christ has made God's sun the very
symbol of that royal freedom of giving which characterizes
the generosity of true love. In its own way, physical light
helps us to comprehend more truly what it means to say
"as God loves." Of all His creations it is the sun whose action symbolizes most eloquently the very qualities of His
heart. Each morning it recalls to us that a Love exists which
does not reject nor refuse, a Mercy that never tires, a Gen-

erosity that always takes the initiative, and a Delicacy so exquisite that, never to frighten those whom it seeks, it hides from them its Face and its Name.

Who would ever think of doubting for an instant the action that light exercises upon him? Everyone willingly recognizes it. And, in so doing, he recognizes that he himself must reckon with another authority than that of his own decisions. So, to this degree at least, light draws from the most proud and the most skeptical such expressions of humility as the finest sermons could not evoke. Unless he is a man of deliberate bad faith, the most hardened positivist is forced to admit that he is conditioned by other causalities than his own.

Daybreak heralds, and even, in a certain measure, opens the door to the awakening of life. It is a mystery, but the fact is there, and this fact only emphasizes our profound precariousness. Real though it may be, our ontological unity is so "contingent" (as the theologians say) that it is incapable of assuring our psychological unity. Our existence is under the sign, not of continuity, but of discontinuity.

At one and the same time we live identical to ourselves from one end of our life to the other, and strangers to ourselves for a good part of our life. Sleep interrupts the conscious possession, presence, and use of ourselves. Willing or not, we are snatched away from ourselves by sleep. Indeed we are forced to admit that this personality of ours, of which we are so proud, is less *given* to us than loaned. Of our own being, of the reality which we are and represent, we are less the masters, the proprietors, than we are provisional users and its regular guests.

Each little nap is a going away, and every awakening is a coming back.

But this return is a premise that is absolutely gratuitous, that nothing inside or outside us postulates. We owe it to some mysterious, generous goodness that we are drawn out of sleep and emerge from this pit where we have temporarily ceased to live, that we come back to our home and find ourselves again, that we regain consciousness and become ourselves again. No man has any right to the day that he rediscovers. And the very fact that he awakens again is a gift, which, from the ontological and biological point of view, is a free gift, the consequence of pure liberality.

Light is the messenger, as effective as it is friendly, of the sovereign goodness upon whose mercy our daily existence depends. Dawn, which introduces us so gently to each day, spares our rudely awakened eyes. It clouds with sweetness and grace whatever this daily initiation into life could hold to frighten us. It offers to our sight a world all new, washed clean of the fatigues of the previous day; and progressively it accustoms us to day again.

The transition accomplished and the adaptation made, little by little the full day communicates its own intensity to living beings. Launched anew by it, their vitality stirs and acts. Each one finds energy again, and his full consciousness of himself, courage and animation, the confidence to speak at full voice, to go and to come, to challenge others, to shout.

A mysterious harmony synchronizes light and the vital spirit; so much so that its waning involves a slowing of action. The decline of the day marks the appearance of fatigue, release from self-mastery and the control of one's own personality. Evening is the time to return to calm, and also the time of weakness. Attention relaxes, mind and heart throw off restraint. It is the time of melancholy and confessions, unburdenings of the heart, confidences. So, secretly counselled, each one consents to be less himself, suddenly disinterested in everything. A strange sense of ease leads him to attach less importance to the things of this world, so desired, so difficult to acquire and bitterly guarded all the day, but of which he knows that in a fleeting moment, sleep—momentarily or forever?—will inexorably despoil him.

Sleep and death! Who does not associate them, even to the point of indicating one by the name of the other— these two states which differ only in their length? Both render us powerless, stripped, and solitary; and their dual mystery, equally obscure, frightens us in the same way.

One and the other, they snatch us away and carry us off. No will and no bonds can resist them. No illusion about them can exist; each one of us must submit to them in an absolute solitude.

We invent a language meant to be reassuring. "To join one another in sleep," "to sleep together." These are absurd phrases. Two people can stretch out side by side, enlaced and united, until the moment when sleep overcomes them, carries them off, and separates them. They have a bed in common, but not their sleep.

Each one, when he goes to sleep, goes again to his own pit where none can follow him. Totally abandoned and unconscious, he falls, plunges, founders into an abyss that engulfs him. Except for some surface ripples we call dreams, he retains nothing of that black lake, full of silence, where thought is abolished and attention is annihilated. No call can reach him there.

Where does he go? Very far, no doubt, since those tireless companions that are pain and care, grief and anguish, lose contact and cease to harry him.

They are waiting for him on his return, but he will find them changed. He emerges and reappears, strangely vitalized, restored, refreshed, relaxed. Why? He does not know. He knows only one thing: sleep's benefit depends on its depth, upon how completely he was stripped of everything, separated from himself, cleansed from all possessions and all people with which the preceding day had burdened him. Could he, of himself, attain this detachment, upon which depends direct contact with the Source? Only sleep, in stripping him bare, prepares him for this mysterious meeting place where, body and soul, living people recover their strength. Wise benefactor, it replenishes best those who know how to empty themselves best, those who are most ready to give themselves up to it, because they are the most detached and the most generous.

He, the shadowy one, leads us to truth about ourselves, forces us to admit our limitations and our powerlessness. Who would dare to have pretensions or pose at omniscience in his presence? His secret, veiled in obscurity and covered by night, eludes all our investigations. It teaches us humility. When we are thinking of ourselves we call it "oblivion," when we are thinking of others, "mystery."

Others, whom we think we know so well, do we even recognize them when we chance to see them sleeping?

You, with whom I live and about whom I know so much —how different you appear to me! From what depths of you emerges this face, so slackened or shrunken, so noble or so weak? Where does this strange breathing come from, which marks a slow rhythm, regular, solemn, in which I cannot find your feverish excitement, your precipitancy, your inconsistency? Your very position, relaxed, passive, fragile, is nothing like you, who are so energetic, so strong, so authoritative, so assured, so disdainful. Are you really the same one? Who are you, you whom I find sleeping, whom I surprise?

I am jealous of this power that can snatch from you what my friendship has not been able to obtain. It takes away my illusions and my security. You tell me that you have confided everything to me. That is not true, for now I see you are quite another person. Everything between us must be questioned. You are restless in your sleep, your lips are moving. What are you saying? What use is it to question you? You do not even hear me!

Who is this being whom I do not know? When is he truly himself—when he is awake, or when he is sleeping?

I do not even dare to summon him, to say to him, "You!" With terror I overhear myself speaking to myself, saying of him there, "He is asleep." I treat him as a stranger, an unknown.

At last comes day, to give me back the one I know, the one I love, with all his vanities and his faults, but also with the face and the gestures, the look and the voice that are familiar to me. Sleep frightens me, for it takes away all that I possess of others.

Nevertheless, we must resign ourselves to sleep. . . . So

I understand why, in the evening, light does not abandon us abruptly. It prepares the night gradually, treats our weary eyes carefully, is gentle to our hearts, which are growing foolish. It watches over us as late as possible. And, in the moment when it finally leaves us, in order to persuade us that in its absence we shall be well cared for, surrounded by a wonderful Attention, it disappears in a warm, tender sunset like the gentle Mercy of God.

The day colors the day's work more than we usually care to admit. Our humor and our output feel the influence of the grayness or the brightness of the sky. In our gaiety or our melancholy, our happiness or our depression, light plays a large part.

Through the years, not only our daily mood but our very temperament comes to reflect the customary light of the land where we live. Minds, characters, tastes, and most of all, the plans we cherish and the works we produce, differ profoundly, depending on whether we live under sunny or cloudy skies.

The ancients have emphasized the importance of this phenomenon better than the positivists. It is striking to note the great and universal importance given by "spiritual" people to solar influence—a point on which our modern materialists, in the name of science, are curiously reticent. The ancients attributed to sunshine and humidity the generation of all inferior creatures. This idea, which we consider naïve, nevertheless shows us the very high opinion the medievalists held of the role of light in the world.

The very duration of the hours of light is rich in implications. It marks the average quantity of energy a living organism can use. The animal world yields itself willingly to this wise regulation. There is no beast that does not get its sleep. We can't say as much of humans, who impose harassing night watches on their bodies. Necessity, uneasiness, eagerness for gain, remorse, and a thousand other reasons make them insensible or strongly resistant to the invitation to sleep when daylight disappears. They ignore or run away from this respite that is so necessary for them.

They imagine that they can prolong the day. Their ingenuity has created admirable artificial lights. But ingenuity has not discovered the secret of proportionally increasing their capacity for work or their resistance. The nervous system will sooner or later suffer very serious consequences from lack of sleep. Its too-delicate texture will not endure being forced. This is the reason for many breakdowns and psychic disorders.

Mental equilibrium demands adaptation to physiological conditions. The alternations and seasonable variations of day and night dictate the limits to the rhythm of which they are capable. In its own domain and its own manner the light of the day instructs us in a realm where instinct is lacking. Too anxious and too excited, we give much less attention to the body's warnings than to signs from outside ourselves. So by its coming and going, light serves as an objective sign marking the length and interval, the division of work and of rest. Even though it comes from so far away, it helps us to synchronize ourselves with this material universe in which we live.

We see here a vague but true sign of the will of God, but this does not keep us from admiring light as such. No one

has more willingly celebrated it than the saints, and it is
very natural that in the Canticle of Creatures the Little
Poor Man of Assisi sings of it, not for the benefits it brings
us, but as a symbol of the glory that it gives to God its
Author:

> Be praised, my Lord, in all Your creatures,
> Especially Sir Brother Sun,
> Who made the day and by whom You
> Give light;
> And it is beautiful and radiant with great splendor,
> Splendor of You, Most High; and it is Your standard-
>   bearer.
> Be praised, my Lord, for our Sister
> The Moon and the Stars,
> In the heavens You have fashioned them, clear and
>   precious
> And beautiful.

2.

Intelligence, the source of vision, is always compared to
light. These two in their functioning and their qualities
have identical attributes. A mind is called clear or foggy,
sparkling or dull; or even, in certain privileged cases, "a
light." Where do we get these comparisons?

The mind is the faculty of discovering and grasping, and
its essential mission is to enlighten its possessor as to the
nature and value of realities. When intelligence is faced
with a fact, it does the same thing for that fact as the light
of day does for visible objects: it shows them to us. Neither
the mind nor the light alters the things they reveal. They
show them to us, show us what they do and what they are.

To this respect for their object both unite a scope of action so wide as to be almost limitless. Light is not diminished by the immensity or complexity of the landscape, nor can the multiplying, extending, and deepening of the fields of knowledge change the receptive capacity or the analytic vigor of the mind. Each one in its own order comes from a source that has inexhaustible potentialities.

But there the comparison must stop. Inanimate light does not understand the spectacles it raises up, whereas intelligence is the living beneficiary of the riches it uncovers. It is both clear light and a luminous look. It takes possession of and retains the object on which it rests. It makes its own the world it travels through. So it never advances without enriching, expanding, or deepening its own interior universe. It carries in itself a world as deep and varied, as sparkling and vast as the whole universe. And it is the quickener and absolute master of this universe. This inner world owes to intelligence both its consistency and its transformations.

That is why we have always held intelligence to be the highest human faculty, the one to which we owe the inward fullness that makes each individual a veritable universe. The philosophers have shown us the importance of this incredible power, but no one, not even a pagan, has dared to exalt it as much as the sacred Psalm revealed by God: "You have printed in us, Lord, the beauty of Thine own Face."

Intelligence makes those who possess it godlike. It confers on them an intellectual stature out of all proportion to their physical relativity and their ontological limits. It allows them to become in spirit all that they are not by nature; to identify themselves with what they are not, to take possession of things which they could not physically or legally possess, to feed themselves with them and treat them interiorly as they like. It confers on them the privilege of a double existence. To natural life, organic or social, it adds another life with riches and intensity that do not depend on exterior resources, but only on the use each one makes of his marvelous powers.

No one can be enriched with this most precious attribute of life except through his own efforts.

So much grandeur is not without its risks. Temptations lie in wait for the man who lets himself be carried away by the intoxication of knowing and the superiority that the power of understanding confers upon him. Then, the spectator transforms himself into a judge, into a sovereign distributor of praise and blame. Listening only to his own opinions, he uses his mind less in trying to understand than in imposing his own decisions upon reality.

He plays at being a demiurge, the molder of the world and the arbiter of values. He confuses his power of forming ideas with that of changing the order of things. So he comes to invent constructs with which perhaps he is fascinated, but to which nothing in reality corresponds: they have the emptiness and the artificiality of mirages engendered by fever or thirst.

Like light, created intelligence is made for discovering realities, not for bringing them into being. The insights of the mind owe their certitude to their content, which depends directly on creative action. Apart from this allegiance, the most gifted intelligence can give only a semblance of life to its own illusions. It only squanders and wastes its wonderful powers.

Morality and religion also have recourse to ideas about light and its action.

The Evangelist St. John made light the very symbol of goodness and faithfulness to God, while shadows represent evil and infidelity. In His preaching, Christ always liked to refer to Himself as "light" rather than to call Himself by the more esoteric name "wisdom": "I am the Light of the world; he who follows Me shall never walk in darkness, but shall have the light of life."

Anyone, no matter how ignorant he is, can understand the symbolism of such words. They speak of the purity of the action of Christ, but also of His depth and His discreet reserve. He does not force the consent of anyone. He proposes the truth with a modesty at least equal to that with which light shows us the splendors of creation. So St. Paul understands it, when he counsels the Christians to be inspired, in their conduct and their plans, by such examples. In fact, this is the way we can recognize authentic charity, which knows how to mix the greatest generosity with the greatest discretion.

There is a still more sublime application of the idea of light: It serves to denote the very perfection of God. To suggest to us the extraordinary, the inconceivable purity of God and the impossibility of comparing it with anything whatsoever here below, St. Paul finds no better way to tell us of it than, "God who dwells in inaccessible light." And the marvel is that we understand how well this image succeeds in suggesting that God is simultaneously the nearest and the farthest from everything existing.

Revelation draws still more from the same image. Jesus has said, "I am the Light of the world"; the Catholic Creed calls Him "Light of Light." By those three words, better than any number of discourses, we understand that what is involved is the very uniqueness and transcendence of the mystery of the fruitfulness of God. An image is enough to make crystal clear that, here, the verb "proceeds" does not change anything of the equality of Persons, and that the distinction of Persons does not imply any difference of nature.

The idea of light is, in truth, at the same time the most universal, the most accessible, and the most perfect. This masterpiece of creation succeeds in imposing itself on all with such clearness that no one is astonished to find it applied to domains infinitely superior to its origin. It is so well fashioned for them that we have some difficulty in remembering its entirely material antecedents.

But what surpasses everything is that light keeps intact its familiar and charming simplicity in the heart of its most sublime transpositions. Clothed by light, the most difficult truth loses its austerity. And, needless to say, we are no longer astonished that God has explicitly claimed it. Light has won more hearts than many of His other attributes.

3.

Vision is a challenge to physical laws: a humble organ takes in the whole universe, brute forces are confronted, yet no injury results.

To what does the eye owe this charmed life? Certainly not alone to the possibilities of the body to which it belongs. The power of the body never goes beyond a restricted field of action. If all our eyes had for their data were what they could gather by our local movements—if that were all—our eyes would be shortsighted indeed. But this is not the case, and in spite of the weight, the weakness, and the slowness of our body, the eyes are endowed with a quickness and a power that we may say are almost limitless. Of all our activities, that of our eyes is surely the one we cannot complain about at all. We indicate this by using expressions reserved for success and ease. We say that our eyes touch, skip, bound, dart, rush, take wing, extend, go beyond.

They always conquer. But they are less the victors than the beneficiaries. They owe the victory to an alliance which, exterior and material though it may be, prepares the work so well for them that they have nothing to do but record its results.

How can we describe the work that light accomplishes, except by saying that it brings together and puts at our doorsteps things that we cannot possibly reach? It resolves problems that would otherwise be insoluble for us, problems of distance and disproportion. It makes possible a kind of contact that avoids the vicissitudes and changes of physical contiguity. Visual grasping does not need organic efforts or moving about in space. It implies something more, something better: a true transfer and an adaptation, of which light alone is capable. Alas, we can better appreciate the results of this tour de force than penetrate its secrets.

I find very natural and effortless a fact that really smacks of the miraculous: without my doing it, without even lifting a hand, the light brings me enormous mountains, innumerable forests, inviolate glaciers, faraway clouds, the magnificent sea. For me it captures the grace of birds, the frolics of fish, the gamboling of wild game. It yields up to me the splendor of scenery and of jewels. It gathers up glances and smiles and confides them to me; it catches up faces and bodies for me. The world that it lightens, it harvests and vintages, all as a gift to me.

Even more than day, night lets me glimpse the glorious performances that this magician accomplishes to overwhelm me. From the far confines of the limitless firmament lights come to me by thousands; and they array themselves in such a way that, in spite of my ignorance, I cannot help appreciating something of the extraordinary travels they must have embarked on before they reached me.

Pascal claimed that he felt frightened before these infinite gulfs of night. Why could he not forget, for a moment, his fixed opinions, his tormenting sadness, his melancholy interpretation of all this grandeur? If he had been less preoccupied with himself, he would have admired more. And perhaps he would have written a marvelous epic of the light.

Unbelievable are the distances crossed, unimaginable the speed, astronomic the duration of the journey—millions of years, sometimes! And yet light comes to us new and pure, and presents us with an image of its radiant source, an image as sharp and as clear as that of the lamp we hold in our hand.

To give us the data from its original source, the light of the stars accomplishes wonders which science can only record without being able to explain. How does this light manage to give us intact the image of its primal home, when, during the thousands and thousands of years, the source has lost its incandescence and reflects only a dead star? One way or another, light must retain the past, since it is capable of restoring it to us with no trouble.

Science tells us that the luminous waves can preserve their integrity because they travel within a system that protects them. They are only a small part of the formidable radiation that the stars send out in melting. These forces, hurled into space, follow trajectories which nothing can throw off the track. But though this explains the way the revealing power of the luminous waves is maintained, it also poses a new problem: how can these frightening forces appear to us as friends?

We know now what sort of cataclysms could provoke a direct astral bombardment. And yet, between us and them watches a Mercy that is always calming and gentling, sifting and decanting these monstrous powers. When they leave a certain zone, only a little way off, their formidable outburst begins to slacken. A sorting takes place among the molecules. And their distribution is so delicately precise that it strips them of all power to harm. Thus the luminous waves, in spite of their prodigious rapidity, touch and penetrate the most fragile tissues of this world without hurting them or affecting their sensitivity.

And just consider the contrast: on one hand we contemplate dramas on so turbulent and astronomical a scale that physics and chemistry can only stammer about them.

Worlds are the theaters and the victims of these tragedies, and immensity the stage. And on the other hand, the light of the stars, soothing, enchanting; the image, in the mind of men, of a tranquil and sure order, limpid as eternal peace. Perhaps the night is so sweet and its light so tender only because they are the very pure essence of the sacrifice of stellar universes without number.

Apart from the impressions it awakens, the light creates a state of fact not permitted by our other natural conditions. What does it matter whether I am here or there, near this or that, and that I can move about but slowly? I have other means than direct contact for reaching things. Light puts marvelous privileges at my disposal. It delivers me from the limitations of slowness. With only one look I can embrace the content of space, attain the heights, range over the fields, survey the sea, overtake the wind, caress a tiger, stride over the clouds, capture the Great Bear, and cruise the Milky Way.

Besides the unlimited enlargement of its field of observation (and the limitless enrichment of these vistas) our vision owes to light its quickness, its promptness. Set free from the slaveries of local locomotion, it is equally free from the duration that measures it. Sight benefits by the nearly instantaneous speed of light. That means that realities and different movements can be present to us before we touch them or mingle with them. Sight foresees physical encounters. Before they touch me or I reach them I have already marked the existence, the nature, the behavior, and the dispositions of the things light shows to me. When they are "there" in virtue of their real presence, local, within reach of word or action, they do not surprise me, and their behavior is not unknown to me. Having grasped them at a distance, I was warned about them and prepared for them.

So I owe to light a vision that escapes from the very limits of physical duration properly so called. It does not know the servitudes and slownesses of progressive succession. It rises above the immediate and narrow limits of the frame in which direct vision is cramped and the data furnished by those events we ourselves have actually experienced.

Neither vision nor the intellectual and affective life it documents and nourishes is conditioned by the situation. It is never true that realities, to interest and enrich us, must touch us or be really seen. Our horizon is infinitely larger than that comprised in the orbit of experience resulting from contacts alone. On the physical plane, physical light introduces contacts and presences—and, through them, spiritual reactions—which, bringing about other results than those due to actual contacts, play an important part. We owe to them the effective power of exercising our transcendence. Without this grasp at a distance, would it be possible to take any initiative whatever? Prisoners of the immediate present, we should be doomed to a behavior consisting only of reflexes as perilous as they would be impromptu.

Light frees us from the narrowness of localization, and

also from chaos and uncertainty. It gives us landmarks more stable and more sure than our next-door neighbor. It allows me to judge the importance of beings according to other criteria than those of the framework in which I am set. If beyond this hill I see only snowy peaks, I make them into a mountain. I owe to light this sense of relativity.

I owe to light also a sense of fixity and regularity. In everything I see change taking place, in a cadence that varies with each one. On what basis can I evaluate modifications, foresee changes, mark and guide myself in the midst of this variety, which is even more complicated than it is admirable? But always, behold, the light of the stars shows me a world whose order never varies, whose visible appearance offers a regularity as exact as a calculation. The starry universe is the only thing that appeases and satisfies the need for certainty. So it has been well taken as a measure of realities here on earth.

It comes from very high and very far, this light that lets us dissipate all shadows, not only those of the physical night, but also those of incoherence and uncertainty. If human knowledge does not refer to the stars in one way or another, and orient itself in the fixed heavens, it can never succeed in freeing itself from the narrowness and pretentiousness of subjectivity.

Immense are the distances that light overcomes. Its wonderful labor is not entirely in vain: many eyes are open to read its messages.

Why do people so often rule out a priori the existence

of any other light? It seems inadmissible to them that, in the purely spiritual order, God can make us capable of leaping to His truth across the abyss that separates His infinity from our minds. Why do they not meditate upon the comparison "Revelation—Light" which is so clearly emphasized in the Bible?

This light is not composed of molecules, but of words, designed to be perceived by our minds. Everyone knows how far the power of words goes beyond their physical text: that words traverse other spaces than those which separate the stars. The distance from one mind to another mind, from one heart to another heart, surpasses—no matter how close they are!—the distances of the stars in the firmament. And yet words travel across them, in spite of, very often because of, obstacles that are inconceivably opaque. Why should God fail, here where the human heart succeeds?

Neither the laws of thought nor those of the heart can allow us to say that supernatural revelation goes against the possibilities and the needs of being. Quite the contrary: the small material particles of which light is composed have been made capable, by God Himself, after they have crossed immeasurable distances for thousands of years, of awakening a marvelously intact vision of their source. Can not the same God initiate us into His secret by charging with an analogous virtue human words already familiar to our minds, near to our hearts?

The blind man who has never known the spectacles light shows us can be forgiven for not daring to believe his ears when stories are told him about it. He is forgiven no longer if, because of his own narrow experience, he calls those who speak to him impostors or dreamers. How can we persuade him? The light is so rich that one cannot explain or defend it by a reality still more beautiful. It is its own unique advocate.

❖

CHAPTER III

Hearing and Listening

1.

IN studying the organ of hearing, the physiologist admires its delicate, complex structure. The most highly perfected kinds of receiving apparatus are feeble imitations of this astonishing instrument, about which most people know little more than its name. Without pretending to the exact knowledge of the anatomist, who can enumerate the many parts of the ear and specify their functions, the layman may at least notice and describe in some detail the advantages a human being gains in the act of hearing.

To hearing we owe the power of capturing sounds from outside, and in this way getting in touch with exterior reality, even if reality is beyond the grasp of touch or even beyond the perception of sight. Hearing makes the universe larger for us and lessens the inconveniences of the limitations the body imposes on us. It makes us conscious that others exist, and not only that they exist, but that they

live, for the sound they make and we hear is truly the
sound of their activities and their movements.

But hearing does not merely perceive; it discerns. Sounds
are not anonymous; mysteriously, they carry with them
something of the extraordinary variety of their causes: the
sound of the fountain is not the sound of the wind, nor the
thump of falling fruit the same as the noise of hail or rain.
The subtle and delicate ear distinguishes these differences,
from a distance, without the aid of sight. The world of
sounds builds up for us the real world, with its hollows, its
heights, its depth, its mass, and its diversities.

The ear seizes not only the distinction, but the value of
this universe. Sounds, like beings, have their density, their
quality, and their timbre; the ear applies to them a palpation that is invisible but sure. Sometimes it draws joy from
them, sometimes suffering; but always knowledge, and
often a more exact knowledge than sight brings. The ear
introduces us to a universe more ethereal and more profound than that of brute bodies; it confers on us a kind of
clarity sometimes more precious than sight can give, because it is more stark and therefore more occupied with
the essential. Blind people offer us an undeniable proof of
this strange clarity: we know that, thanks to their hearing,
they are so open to the most intimate core of beings that
we judge them—and they think themselves—less unhappy
than the deaf, whose infirmity makes them prisoners inside
themselves, isolated for life.

We can appreciate the social advantages of the power
of hearing; but this does not mean that we try to use it to
the best advantage. We make a strictly utilitarian use of
it. No one ever thinks of cultivating and sharpening his

hearing. Yet it opens an unlimited horizon to us. The world of sounds reaches very far, very high; indeed, its immense reach goes to the very limits of the physical universe, with its all-radiating sonic vibrations.

But the ear receives this sonorous message in its original freshness, with meek obedience. Although the mind, under the influence of previous knowledge and preconceived ideas, often misshapes the data presented to it, hearing registers purely and simply what it hears. It is a marvelously objective faculty, and that is why it has so much to give us.

Let us not, however, think of it as strictly passive, like the instruments, recently invented, that are limited merely to recording what strikes them. The ear has a very varied reception to offer to sounds. It shrinks from discordances, but submits to them. Harmony makes it expand and become more attentive—and this quite spontaneously. There is no man in the world capable of resisting a word or a musical note that can fulfill the need of harmony that his ear requires. So, all through the ages, music has been considered an educative art and the best possible appeal to action; it possesses the privilege, as sovereign as it is mysterious, of instantly catching and holding the attention of human beings.

Before explaining the role of hearing in musical perception we must speak, at least briefly, of its place in human relations. We can quickly sum up its importance: it is the proper agency of the grasp of language.

Although speech belongs to the domain of physical vibrations and is made up of the same waves, no person considers it an ordinary sound. It constitutes a world apart. Articulated, distinctly pronounced, it is not in the least like the cries that animals and even man himself utter under the influence of one emotion or another—however varied such sounds may be. The division and cadence of speech are quite unlike those of music or singing. When we try to explain it, we cannot analyze the process of speaking. Speech makes use of the very same organs that permit us to cry out or to sing. The breath of the lungs, the vibratory cords of the larynx, the sounding-box of the mouth, the muscles of the tongue and the lips are distinguished in mankind only by a greater refinement and flexibility. No, it is not a question of the organs involved; rather, of the one who makes the sound, when sound is made to transmit impulses much less elemental and instinctive than those of fear or joy, hunger or desire. And, too, the very quality of these organs would lead us to guess that their object is not merely physiological.

In truth, the final secret of speech lies outside the body; it lies in the influence, which we cannot deny, of the spiritual soul over the flesh. No where else can we better appreciate the extent of this mastery. Man uses the physical possibility of speech and self-expression so much at his whim and with such ease that he makes no distinction between the difficulties of inward and outward utterance. The qualities of one depend upon the qualities of the other.

But what good is this marvelous power of expressing oneself if there is no one to listen? With no ears, who would wish for speech? It would be only sterile chattering, a monologue as unsatisfactory as the cry of a bird lost in space or an animal strayed in the desert. Here we put our finger on the most thrilling service rendered to us by our power of hearing: it delivers us from solitude, and allows us to hear one another, to join and comprehend one another.

As generous as it is, sight cannot reveal to us what is going on in the depths of another person, the complexity of his thoughts and his desires, the secret of his personality. To see a person existing and acting teaches us relatively little about him. Things unseen carry the discoveries of sight to infinity. Each one bears within himself an immense universe. He alone explores it; he alone grasps it; he alone knows it; and he alone can tell of it. He expresses himself to himself and to others; and then, when we listen to him, we learn about him. Between the mouth that proffers it and the ear that hears it, speech, tenuous and fragile, creates a miraculous tie; by it, in fact, two spiritual universes—more irreconcilable and more distant, in spite of their likeness, than two stars—enter into contact. If they could not speak and hear, men would live side by side without ever really meeting or explaining things to one another.

So we can understand the importance men attach to all that has to do with expressing and comprehending thoughts and feelings. It is through hearing that they mutually approach one another and enrich one another. Hence the care to adjust and accustom the ear to the sounds proper to language, without which speech would be only an indecipherable murmur.

To the man who knows how to listen, human speech yields something more than the message intended by the one who speaks; and this something lies not in the nature

of his utterances, his eloquence, or the intensity of his de-
livery, but in the very quality of his voice. Even more than
the sense of the words and the manner of saying them, the
quality of the voice reveals the quality of the soul.

Whether we wish it or not, a relationship exists between
the mind and the body, a certain community of vibrations
and rhythm which, unknown to us, shows in the outward
behavior. Inevitably, a face, a look, a bearing, above all a
voice, betray the secret of the soul by which they live.

If an ear is ever so little attentive, it recognizes at once,
in sensing the "grain" of a voice, the feebleness or force,
the pride or weakness, the nobility or vulgarity of the
speaker. Perverted though it may be, a soul is rarely so
much at its ease in evil as not to show it naturally: by
almost imperceptible signs—uneasiness in his glances, a
slight awkwardness in the voice—a vigilant observer recognizes, or at least guesses, the intrusion of a perverse will.

These give us nothing but vague indications and obscure
presentiments; they cannot support or justify exact judgments. But we cannot completely deny the importance and
significance of such imponderables. Surely, oftener than the
critical examination of what a speaker is actually saying,
this "sense of the voice" helps the listener to find beneath
the words the deep resonance of the real self.

2.

Besides human speech, and beyond it, rise myriad strata
of sounds that also strike the ear. But they are not all
beautiful. The ear surrenders only to sounds that have the
power to seduce it. That is why music can penetrate into
us and influence our feelings and, through them, the mind
and heart.

to its likeness the substance of sound—the most supple and malleable of existing substances, because it is the most subtle. Music arranges and transposes sound as it pleases, confers on it the tonality and modality of its choice; simplifies or complicates it as seems best; makes it into an austere chant or an orchestrated *tutti*. There is no kind of sound that music does not make use of: produced by a violin or a horn, by a flute or an oboe, by a bassoon or piano, the same note is not the same. The chosen instrument renders it delicate or sharp, mellow or harsh, tender or rough, warm or dry.

The musician is master of the choice of his notes, of their combination and the quality of their sound; their cadence and succession depend only on him. In such conditions, how can music help being the richest and most flexible of all means of expression? Modulating itself to all feelings, it surrounds us and invades us on all sides.

So we understand why musicians have made it convey such different messages. Not that they intend it to express a dialectic that would be as explicit and exact as discursive reasoning or as sharply defined as speech; but a message awakening in another an inward climate, a state like those they feel themselves. With this intention, many composers have tried to give to their works a title explaining what they thought they had expressed and wished others to find there. This is a legitimate aim, but, to some extent, gratuitous, because the radiation and atmosphere proper to music depend less on formulae borrowed from reasoning than on the texture, tempo, and the tonality of the composition itself; and it is to these that the true lover of music devotes himself. The really great composers know this;

determined to keep their art entirely pure, they explain nothing of their intentions and remain content to indicate the key and time of their compositions, which they then christen with a humble numeral—the "opus number."

Such discretion is wise, moreover, for the personal dispositions of the listeners influence greatly the attention and the interpretations they give to music. Our actual state profoundly conditions our vision and our hearing, our feelings and appreciations. But music is so subtle and varied that it very rarely leaves us indifferent. Its variety and versatility allow it to insinuate itself into us, to lend its coloration to the landscape of the soul, and, giving a voice to the indistinct and confused murmurs of the impulses pressing in upon us, it reveals to each one of us the meaning it carries. We feel in our hearts the boundless sweep of the words of Baudelaire:

Music often takes me like a sea.

We must confess that musical emotion often surpasses the theme that provokes it. The inward temper lends itself to a certain piece, and the impression we retain surpasses in quality and depth the actual efficacy of the music that occasioned it. Here, the work benefits by the dispositions we have at the moment. We expect something of a certain kind, and here, from the first measures, the atmosphere and pace of the piece, reaching within us down to the zone already prepared for it, are enough to overwhelm us. Our interior song, suddenly liberated, rises up to meet the outward song, or even to substitute for it almost without our knowing it. We are moved and excited, but perhaps mostly by our own selves. The music has been only the pretext and the occasion. So it is that many facile or senti-mental pieces of music touch us only because of the com-plicity of certain feelings in ourselves. Pure beauty of har-mony and true musical perfection count for nothing in the emotion that they cause; all that matters is the more or less conscious excitation of feelings which these compositions have awakened.

Great music, the sovereign music of the masters, is quite another thing. It does not move us by flattering us, but— a very difficult thing—by imposing itself on us and taking us out of ourselves. It, and it alone, has the mysterious golden key that sets free our sense of beauty, sometimes padlocked so strongly in the deepest place of our heart. Let certain works be repeated, and soon something rises in us that we had forgotten or disdained. So distracted, so tormented, and so weak, we do not recognize ourselves; a new spirit crops out in us, a serenity we did not remember is reborn, and a taste for purity pervades us. So we listen to certain passages of Beethoven, all the works of Bach, all those of Mozart, and still others that we all know. We listen, and another world opens up. It is not the sea, tumul-tuous and violent, colorful and clamorous, which takes us, but a limpid fountain murmuring, a calm sky unveiled, an angel's wing brushing us. We listen a long while, a long while . . . and when it is all over, we seem to wake from a dream.

What is the secret of such music? Why is it such a talisman? Vainly, through the centuries, have men sought to elucidate the mystery. No one knows the magic formula, the golden number that gives a work the sovereign force to awaken and set free the best in our hearts. We cannot deny that such a power exists, but we cannot explain or understand this gift. The best-informed musical critic must abdicate in its presence. The critic certainly can explain formulas and laws, techniques and procedures, but like the biologist in the presence of life, the critic sees the final secret of the genius elude his analysis. Like life, musical success guards its mystery perfectly. The *note bleue*, which represented for Chopin the supreme achievement of a work, is beyond all technique and all artifact: it is the free and unpredictable crown given to composers without their knowing why.

We see it lavished on works that seem to show no skill nor learning; such sometimes are the simple songs that brave the centuries, or melodies that we feel from the first are imperishable. So many productions, on the other hand, are more skillfully and knowingly wrought, yet touch us only superficially. The angel of music has failed to bless them. Why? It is a mystery!

Perhaps they were too pretentious, and their authors had forgotten the road to the true wellsprings. Song is born of life, not merely of inventiveness or even of talent; only the humble perceive it. The greatest masters knew this, and so we see that they never lose contact with that inexhaustible mine of rhythm and melody—the songs of the land. In France and Germany, in Italy and Spain, in Belgium and America, the best composers have drawn their purest inspirations from this source. They recognize that this naïve music is less the child of the brain than of life; and the most intense labor, the most advanced technique are nothing if the soul is lacking. The soul . . . that is, the song that finds the road to the heart, the song that suits the ear, the song which, through all refinements, demands above all else this one thing—to hear the "note" that makes it listen, and draws it out of somnolence and distraction, away from banality and vulgarity: the note awakening purity, mastery, triumphant freedom of a being in tune with itself, the messenger of joy, recalling that it comes "from somewhere else."

What does it matter whether this note is simple or complex, a song spoken or mimed! The essential thing is that it has received the approbation of the humble people, who are more infallible judges than the professors. A work can begin around it and counterpoint be erected upon it, but the composer has a duty to respect it. On this condition, his work will retain the best of its first freshness, and everyone's ear will accept it. In music, as in all human productions, the first note is the basis of the subject. Here intuition is the happy surprise of the ear, the instinctive agreement with whatever overwhelms the natural attention of the hearer. However complex and highly evolved he may become, the composer remains a man; that is, one who is hungry for what he most lacks—simple and pure harmony. This alone is heard by the man whose works are inspired by a great respect for the heart's hope.

The world into which the universe of sounds introduces us is, then, as immense as it is marvelous, and it is ours without any effort on our part—except to listen. Yet it is not the only world by any means. Beyond music or speech begins another domain, still richer and more secret. Before they speak or sing, beings exist and live. Silently. To listen to such silence demands a very pure ear, a desire that is virginal in its intensity and truth. But it supposes, previously, the reception and the hearing of song and of speech, direct messengers from the ineffable. Without them, would it still be given us to see the other face of Reality? They are the inevitable, necessary cause of the first contacts. But, faithful and honest, they efface themselves before the thing they adumbrate: the true mystery of the heart and soul, the invisible world.

Thanks to song and to speech, another contact can be initiated—contact with the presence that reaches into the true depths of beings and the mystery of persons. Then love realizes its work, which is not to listen or to speak, but to be there, together, attached to one another, at the same time both unveiled and secret. We recognize all great love by this: that it accepts being silent, nourishing itself with mystery. So is the love of friend for friend, and the love of the soul for God—at the heart of a contemplation that does away with all need for words.

In this the power of listening is consummated and perfected, when love, carried to the limits of what can be learned from words or music, demands to see what signs cannot evoke. And it is by the quality of transmitted silence that the heart finally recognizes the true fullness of the being to which it has given itself.

CHAPTER IV

"Hinder Not Music"

SOMETIMES the words of poets mean more than the speeches of scholars. Such are those which Maeterlinck puts on the lips of old Arkel in *Pelléas and Mélisande*, and whose poignant charm the music of Debussy imparts so well:

> The human soul is very still . . . it suffers so timidly.

It is true that we know almost nothing of ourselves, of what goes on in the depths of us, and our soul is a mystery to us. But this soul is the best part of us, the most precious of all realities, and the one with which the heart is most occupied. What use is it to know the body if the soul eludes us? When we cherish someone, we are on the watch for the secret of his soul, interested in its least manifestations, sensitive to its most subtle echoes. We capture and examine them in hope of knowing the pulsation of their mysterious source. They alone can teach us what goes on in its depths. So it is, then, that if we really want to meet one another heart to heart, and not simply to live beside someone, we have to understand the real value of the means of expression at our disposal.

The easiest source to get at and the one most current is speech, the word translating the thought—that is, what a man can know and explain about himself and others. Speech is precious and fruitful. But when it comes to telling us about ourselves, it leaves us unsatisfied. Its very precision, which makes it the ideal instrument of clear thought, makes it unsuitable for profound confidences. It is too plain, too sharply defined, to contain the so restless and various, so vague and so vibrant soul. What verbal formula could contain something that keeps bursting its bonds on all sides?

Although speech may be very eloquent, still it leaves in the shadows the principal thing of all: the fire that endlessly springs up within us, the currents and eddies, flux and reflux that ceaselessly stir us. But this interior world—most intimate and true—would remain ever inarticulate if there did not exist another means of expression, beyond speech and completing it, one less explicit perhaps and less sublime, but infinitely nearer to the real vibration of life: Music.

Music, like speech, passes through our lips, but it does not first submit to the alchemy of precise reasoning. It is the direct and instinctive expression, as it were a spontaneous modulation, of the true inward vibration. Flowing and supple, moving and nuanced, it projects outwardly this silent motion. Subtle and ephemeral, it is an echo that brings a message, for through it passes the vibrating emotions of the heart. Speech decants and interprets, but music lets us perceive and almost touch the sounds of ineffable regions.

Speech and song! They are two great means by which men confide in one another, two social ties which, when the voice interprets them, permits minds to communicate, souls to unite, and love to be realized and to speak.

This is enough to prove their importance forever. There is no man who is not, to some extent, in tune with music and speech. They are the surest way to reach through to others. The man who knows how to speak and the man who knows how to sing have the key to hearts. They can be sure that others will cleave to them, better than by using heroic gestures or force of arms to win them. Indeed, he alone can convey joy or sadness, peace or trouble; for unlike gestures that are only superficial, speech and music break through the frontiers of the soul at the first attack.

The Church knows their strange power very well. So she has made these two things her principal helpers in her mission of education. She asks speech to convey to minds the divine Truth itself. To music she entrusts the accompaniment of prayer, not by means of superficial gilt-plating or gift-wrapping, but as a stimulus. In music, ethereal and alive, she sees the most effectual and pure rapport between the best of man's feelings and the very life of his spirit. Physically captured and occupied by beauty, the man who sings prays best.

If this were not so, music would not contribute to the integration of the heavy human machine. And this truth obliges us to enter further into its secrets.

Although it may be sensuous in effect, music is not just another expression of the life of the soul. It exacts conditions that guarantee its existence and its worth. Just as speech is not worthy of the name unless a correct and vital thought substantiates it, so also music is truly music only to the degree that whatever it expresses has certain qualities. Beauty from without presupposes beauty within. Beauty here means harmony and accord—that is, harmony which, in the mind and heart, means order and nobility. This is not only the value of music, but its reason for being.

Music is not a banal assembly of sound. Neither the quantity nor the material quality of the elements composing it is the chief thing. The richness and mellowness of its texture, the power and novelty of its movement, would be nothing if there were no law to set them in order and animate them. This discipline alone assures the balance and the integrity of the music, and makes an intelligible ensemble. Without it, conflicts would ravage the work; the proportions would be false and the incoherencies intolerable, and the time, unregulated, would not be cadence nor melody.

Reason alone cannot give the formula of this mysterious thing without which it is not music at all. Logic has no part in it—at least not pure reasoning. Exact rhythm and correct arrangement arise from a more subtle domain whose unity has nothing rigid about it. Although it cannot be reduced to the order of pure mathematics nor formulated in precise rules, the order existing here is nevertheless strict.

Music, like life, is wise but unguessable, coherent though capricious; like life, it cannot, under pain of death, violate the laws that assure its continued existence. If they are delivered to anarchy, living cells die and disintegrate. Left to themselves, without control, sounds produce only something hideous.

Spontaneity alone is not enough. In music as in everything else, a work is beautiful (that is, harmonious) only when its creators and executors tender a humble reception to the laws of order. But the nature of music is such that the musician must add a true asceticism of soul to the discipline of technique. So the "demon" who instructed Socrates summed up all morality in this beautiful advice: "Socrates, make music." Make your entire life a work of beauty, conforming in all things to correct balance. Let your soul and your heart, your mind and your senses be ordered and integrated so that they compose a living harmony. There is no witness more sublime to the deep identification of music with order, which alone can give birth to wise and exact melody and to the blessed plenitude of rhythm.

A musical work, then, is not just a contrivance. Neither hand nor reason nor vital richness nor skill plays the most important part in it. It is a subtle creation, and the elegance and grace of its living architecture depend, above all, on the interior qualities of the one who produces it. First of all there is a certain silence, which suggests that the composer is not to be entirely invaded and overrun by the tumult and disorder of the passions. Such recollection is to music what meditation is to speech—its home and true source.

Numerous and incoherent are the noises within and without. Innumerable are the echoes of the passions. Voices and rumors, crashes and murmurings that are not equally melodious assail our ears. Before expressing any of them, the artist must discern and choose. But to hear them and judge them in terms of beauty, he must get at a distance from them; this is meditation, contemplation. Inspiration is not abandon; and the quality of the artist's inward silence is the most important thing in creating music.

The choices he makes develop directly from his needs and his tastes in beauty. In spite of him, the very nature of the songs he retains announces the predilections of his heart. A superficial soul retains only facile cadences, those most concerned with peripheral reactions and emotions. A passionate and violent man echoes the tumult and the storm. A delicate soul hears and gives back only those things that suit his refinement. A noble, serene soul closes himself to all noise so that he can listen and grasp the song at the very frontiers of his mind and heart, at its most secret and deep moment, at its source. As if beyond himself, he hunts at the heart of purity and of the night for the imperceptible, the capricious, rustling breeze from the heights.

But whatever kind of music is chosen, true music, because of its discipline and harmony, is never without a minimum of nobility and purity. There is a line it dares not cross, abysses to the depths of which it cannot descend. Made of invisible and imponderable things, music, of all the arts, is the most subtle and most inviolable. Harsh and vulgar grossness can have no part in music. Even the most passionate, the most visceral music has something ethereal about it. Without his suspecting it, even the most corrupt musician is always drawn away from the troubled zones of the flesh, by his very art itself.[1]

Using different words from ours, philosophers of other days have very judiciously emphasized the essentially purifying role of music as such. They speak of the purgation of passions (those feelings that have such deep roots in us) only because they know how completely this art mobilizes our whole attention.

Music is made differently from the way we make other things. To make a bridge or a speech means to exercise the hands or the mind, and the soul may be far away. Music is not like that. It occupies us entirely, for in its technical qualities it requires the communion and harmonization of the heart with the sense of beauty. Without this inward awakening to the world of rhythm there is no possible initiation, production, or listening to music. We do not make music unless we live it. And at the same time we give ourselves up to harmony.

That is why the ancients symbolized its power in the myth of Orpheus charming the wild beasts. By music, wild beasts just as dangerous as those of the forests are, if not wholly tamed, at least quieted. Stripping it of its fabulous orchestration, the Church has taken over the pagan's confidence in this art. Of all human manifestations, music is certainly the one Catholicism respects most highly. Rarely

---

[1] From an equal degree of morbidity, a musical theme and a literary theme have different results. The imagination and the thought dwell upon a written theme; there is time for the morbidity to take root. By its very movement, musical orchestration, even the most equivocal, stirs the emotions only momentarily.

in the course of history have measures been taken against musicians. Their very vocation, entirely concerned with order and harmony, preserves them from excessive short-comings of taste. So, in the Church, whatever their personal beliefs were, they have always felt at home.

In their favor the Church goes so far as to relax her disciplinary severity a little. Not without reason, for she knows the incoercible upward strength of music. Whatever the artist may be, he speaks to men in a language that carries them above what can be seen, touched, and felt. Of course this is not yet pure spirituality, but we can readily see that a being impregnated with pure harmony according to human norms is disposed to desire the knowledge of still more beautiful harmonies. Beyond the world of sounds lives the Fullness, silent and sovereign, of whom created chords are but a feeble echo: infinite Wisdom of which it is written, "It disposes all with order, weight, and number." Of this living Harmony, the harmonies here below offer only approximations. Some are immobile and others moving; some closed, others open. Mounting perennial and serene, music has—in the psychological and metaphysical sense of the word—the disarming privilege of awakening in the depths of hearts a homesickness for Him whom a great mystic has called "the silent concert, the resounding solitude."

Better even than the demon of Socrates, the word of Scripture: "Hinder not music!" is at the same time a consecration and a program of action.[2]

Hinder not music, written in life, welling up in your soul; do not hush its song. Do not stop people from singing, for God's work is harmony. In its subtle delicacy, music incarnates one of the highest functions of man; by it, beauty unformed and silent, after having passed through a living heart, becomes to human ears a message of brotherhood, and to the ears of God, an act of thanksgiving and praise.

CHAPTER V

❖

Perfumes and the Sense of Smell

THE SENSE OF SMELL, more humble than sight or hearing, is not one of the major senses to us, as it is to animals; we attach only slight importance to the sensations it produces. To appreciate it correctly we must compare the creatures possessing it with those deprived of it; only then do we see the extent of the field of investigation it covers. It is an awareness without direct contact, detection at a distance, a quicker and more effective perception than that bestowed upon inferior creatures. Of our physiological capital it makes up a much less ordinary element, since its proper activity has deeper and more powerful repercussions on our behavior than we usually suspect.

1.

The sense of smell has for its organ an appendage which, we must admit, makes us smile: the nose. The poor organ cannot help its situation; located in full face and projecting

76

forward, it cannot avoid being seen and—criticized! Its least faults are exposed in full daylight. But this does not keep it from being a good and faithful servant, valiantly performing its duties. Beautiful or not, it exposes itself openly. Nothing protects it. There are no eyelids in whose shadow it can take shelter. It does not work in the hollow of a warm retreat, as does the tympanum; it must confront the rigors of the outside world directly.

Its owner is not happy in these unwelcome circumstances. He is often angry with its questionable shape and still more so with its maladies! The least irritation of the nose plunges us into bad humor. Is there anyone who does not feel ridiculous when he has a heavy cold? To sneeze, to use a handkerchief, are disgraceful gestures for which we must make an apology. Like all humble things, the nose has its share of misfortune. Yet the nose is necessary; and it has not the exclusive responsibility for the ugliness of a face: "A big nose never adorned a beautiful face!" Its malformations, after all, are less serious than its total absence, which would make hideous even the most graceful visage.

Indispensable, by its presence, to the ordering of a face, the nose is still more indispensable, by its good functioning, to the balance of health. The least thing wrong with it has a serious effect on respiration and voice and song—to say nothing of the power to smell. And this makes us give it its due.

As to the rest, current language—that of good sense!— does not fail to mention it. The nose is even made the symbol of sagacity. "He has a good nose" means discernment, judicious clairvoyance; the most precious qualities of the mind. "He has not a good nose," or, "He lacks flair" [1] express the absence of judgment, unskillfulness, the lack of foresight. "He is led around by the nose" tells of a lack of initiative and character. To put someone's nose to the grindstone, to turn up your nose at something, to look down your nose, not to see what is under your nose—all these expressions would make no sense if people were not conscious of the part played by the sense of smell.

In a more precise usage, we see that philosophic language, cautious in its handling of the data of good sense, employs the word *to sense* (Fr., *sentir*) which originally meant *to smell*, for the activity of other organs as well. For, in olfactory perception, the true characteristics of all sensation appear to a typical degree: a living contact with another thing, a kind of penetration of the reality of a subject, the subject itself yielding up its own data to the degree that it is investigated.

The sense of smell has the privilege of perceiving what takes place, at the very moment when it experiences the action of its object: odors. Even when I happen to take no notice of the shapes or colors the daylight reveals to me, or to pay no attention to the noises that break out around me, I take account almost immediately of any odor that makes its way to me. The reaction of the sense of smell seems even quicker and more complete than that of other senses that are certainly superior to it.

To this quickness is added depth; the olfactory memory bears witness that its tenacity and freshness put it in a class apart. An odor strikes us suddenly—and awakens in

[1] Translator's note: The word "flair" has been adopted into English and is correctly used in several senses derived from its French meaning: "*Flair*: n.m. (hunt) scent. *Il a le flair*: He knows how to find out things. *Flairer*: to smell, to scent, to detect. *Flairer quelque chose*: To smell a rat."

us confusedly at first, then more and more precisely, the certainty that we have met it before. But where? We never hunt long for it. "That is it"—the scent of the old home of our infancy, of a room, of a garret, of a garden; that of a dear one whose face and voice have long been buried in the most inaccessible parts of ourselves, which we had tried in vain to recall, and now surging up again, intact, overwhelming! How many times is it not a whiff of an odor that transports us into former times, living something again in all its enrapturing sweetness or atrocious bitterness as if nothing had ever taken place since? There is no need to call on Baudelaire to know that

> Sometimes one finds an old flagon which calls to mind
> Whence gushed out all living a soul which came back . . .
> Here is the intoxicating memory which hovers
> In the troubled air; the eyes close; dizziness
> Seizes the conquered soul and crushes it in both hands.

The memory of odors often conditions the memory of colors and of sounds: undeniable proof of the depth to which what we have breathed in has penetrated into us, although at the moment we attached little importance to it. Of all our complex memories the details that strike us most forcibly at the moment do not play a major part. Of beings and things met, those most fleeting and least solid remain the least perishable: the odor.

2.

Odors belong to the physical world, but their exact nature is far from being perfectly known. Although in recent years science has succeeded in learning the laws of the vibrations of light and sound, which are more subtle, it still keeps silent about the laws of odors. No apparatus has yet been discovered for isolating, dissecting, measuring, and analyzing them.[2] Reason and calculation ought to abandon the attempt to seize and appreciate them. They remain, in the literal sense of the phrase, a pure question of *flair*.

But the vibrations of fragrance are coarser than the waves of light or sound. They consist of an emanation of the very substance of the body—which proves that the outward projection of the corpuscles composing them cannot go on indefinitely. To the extent that it scatters its scent abroad, a body loses its richness and vigor. The appearance and increase, the lessening and cessation of an odor are strictly correlated with the vitality or degeneration of its source. This strict relationship explains why we always speak of an odor as a living reality: it is born and acts, languishes and dies.

But the nature of odors keeps its secret. Entirely physical though it is, the production of odors follows different laws from those ruled over by material forces. No odor arises from a powerfully radioactive body; but a humble flower or a tiny drop of perfume project around them a vast ambient of fragrance.

The burden of weight seems to have no hold on this impalpable scent. It mingles with the thin air. At the mercy of the winds, it remains stagnant or flies away, stops or travels, always light and invisible. It impudently braves

[2] Translator's note: My attention has been called to the recent research of Dr. Hainer, Dr. Emslie, and Miss Jacobson on the problem of smell. It seems that each nostril has a lobe made up of 1,900 glomeruli, and from each, twenty-four nerve fibers go to the brain. With these twenty-four neurons it is possible to get 16,000,-000 different patterns, corresponding to that many odors. So we see that science marches on. Père Boulogne gave up too soon.

space, cold, and heat. At incredible distances, beasts and men can receive the quintessence of faraway sources, enriched with the scent of the lands they have crossed.

Each thing that gives off a smell has its own way of secreting the effluvium: so with flowers, animals, the earth, humans. But the marvel of marvels is that most odors have so marked a personality that we can recognize them at first sniff. Some of them, it is true, are diffused and complex: the scent of the countryside, or of a riverbank; the scent of morning or evening, of a field soaked in sunshine or of underbrush after a storm; the perfume of spring or summer, autumn or winter; the "bouquet" of dry air or humid, of freshness or decrepitude, of life and of death; the odors of the desert and of the city, of the mountains and of the sea.

They all rise, vibrant, mingling with the air. Some travel far, others attach themselves to a house or rest in the hollow of a vale. But we should be entirely ignorant of this symphony and this dance in the sun, light and varied, invisible and untiring, if the sense of smell did not allow us to grasp and interpret them.

Thanks to smell, the air that we breathe is never anonymous. To the extent that we breathe it in, the olfactory papillae touch and savor it. Whether they take pleasure in it or not, they capture and feel the effluvia contained in the air we inhale. They do not take the initiative in this inquiry, nor do they obtain the reward; their reactions are only the result of the quantity of odors the air carries. How can we fail to admire the sureness and delicacy of this living laboratory? Its swift, silent work produces in us a discernment and an awareness which, blind though it be, leads to almost infallible certainties.

Even before we perceive the thing from which an odor emanates, the sense of smell has already detected and even recognized it—and this so keenly that in beasts it attains to a true foreknowledge. Scent is the most disinterested and the surest guide and help to their instinct of self-preservation: it warns them of the dangers they run; of the approach of prey; informs them of the quality of their food or of the herbs they ought to taste; signals the presence of water; leads them unfailingly to their refuge; makes them know their companions or their master. The sense of smell in animals conditions their reflexes of confidence or fear, of friendship or anger. Its role is of vital importance to them.

Although it does not attain such powers of divination, or show it in the same way, the human sense of smell has equally important consequences. The sensations it produces enter into the secret life of motives and desires, expectations and remembrances born of other sensations, which prepare the reactions of the mind and of the will. The impression of odors is added to all these to waken or stimulate, act upon and color them, after their own fashion. Hence these undefined resonances of the least sensation, which Baudelaire has well described:

> As long echoes which from afar are mingled
> In a shadowy and profound unity
> Vast as night or day,
> Perfumes and colors and sounds reply to one another.

That is why, instead of being content to classify odors as useful or noxious, agreeable or unpleasant, we should go back to more complex and carefully graduated divisions, taking account of the echoes and interior eddies each one of them arouses.

The inward echoings of a perfume are difficult to describe exactly: in a kingdom where imponderables rule, rational categories have no place. Sensitivity to perfumes depends on their quality, but still more on the aptitudes of each man and the way he feels at the moment. But let us try to indicate—at least in summary—some of the impressions felt on contact with a beautiful perfume. The first reaction is one of happy relaxation and true delight. While a disagreeable odor makes us, if not actually hold our noses, at least reduce our breathing as much as possible, a perfume always produces the opposite effect. We become greedy gourmands, thinking of nothing but savoring each indrawn breath, to fathom it and take it in again. So we make ourselves willing accomplices of the perfume, helping it to insinuate itself into our own depths. Careful not to lose contact with it, we cling to it, breathing it and sensing it, as if to profit by it as much as possible. It is especially because we attach ourselves to it that it captivates us.

A beautiful perfume, we admit, conquers us; and we are even more sure that it will never arouse our distaste. Nothing is alarming about it; all is so inoffensive, silent, discreet. How can we call it an intrusion, when the visitor is as fragile as it is charming? Yet we are in its power! It needs only to present itself to bewitch us. Breathing it in, we are permeated with its tone and its atmosphere. So it comes to color our inward surroundings, to create in us a climate according to its nature, where thoughts and desires bearing its mark can germinate and grow. While it charms us, a perfume also succeeds in weakening or troubling us, exciting us or lulling us to sleep.

It should not be so astonishing, then, that ever since the world began people have sought to exploit the art of perfume and to cultivate its science, both for pleasure and for profit. The skillful use of perfumes permits of a siege and assures a conquest just as effective and profound as those accomplished by armed strategy, brute force, or a calculating and tricky mind. Hence the importance of perfumes in sacred and profane history: it is not only Christianity that has used perfumes. We are surrounded by scents as diverse as they are unexpected. To understand all this, we must first consider the reason why people use them in ordinary life. Insofar as we can make classifications in such a subject, we can perhaps divide these reasons into three groups, different but complementary: utilitarian, psychological, and symbolical.

Prose precedes poetry, and the pragmatic precedes the pleasant. We should not be surprised, then, to see that man first concentrated his efforts in fighting against bad odors. Not being able to suppress them, he opposed violent perfumes to them. This was a war of counteroffensive, where in the shelter of invisible ramparts a man could brave the fetid exhalations of the places he passed through.

We still exploit the seduction of perfume. Its attraction invites those who pass and whom it strikes to devote a moment to it, to slow their steps, even to stop. Managers of shops know this: they watch over the air their customers breathe, to coax them and make them stay. We all know the extra profit made by a product that is agreeably perfumed. Whether it is a question of useful products or luxury goods, a good smell plays a capital role. Even more than the quality, or the elegance of the package, the delicacy of the scent of merchandise exercises a decisive influence on buyers. The publicity agent who shall one day invent a sweet-smelling handbill will make a fortune.[3]

These very commonplace facts help us to grasp the part smell plays in our appreciations and our choices. An agreeable perfume always disposes us favorably. That is why it has such an important part in the life of a woman.

> I was present like an odor whose insidious depth cannot be elucidated.—Valéry

Neither caprice nor coquettishness—superficial sentiments at best—is enough to explain the innate taste of women for perfume and their disconcerting skill in using it. This comes less from deliberate personal choice than from an essential femininity and a secret conspiracy. Only a profound correspondence between feminine nature and the resources of perfume can explain the eternal, invincible fidelity vowed by women to this instrument of domination.

[3] *Translator's note:* It has already been invented and is in use—in America, at least.

The most dictatorial laws, the warnings of outraged moralists, have never changed them in the least in this respect and never will, come what may. One cannot fight against an attraction so deeply rooted in nature.

Whatever feminists and suffragists say, a woman who is truly feminine knows by instinct that her vocation is not to enter into rivalry with the stronger sex. A certitude more powerful than all words persuades her that her physical forces and her intellectual talents will allow her only the smallest chance of imposing herself upon masculine attention by any striking masterpiece of art or literature. She would be successful there only if her good sense shows her that those whom she dazzles in this way either admire her as confrère and comrade—and never as woman—or they are jealous of her and treat her as a bluestocking. Feminists sick for emancipation protest that they do not care if they are scorned; they think that their social success is enough compensation. But a woman who is truly a woman knows very well that the most perfect intellectual equality in the world would not appease or fill her empty heart or the hunger to be noticed, considered, chosen, and loved for herself, and not for what she contributes or what she accomplishes. She does not feel the need for admiration or for consideration, but for a support and a tenderness attracted by her own self.

And in order to gain these, instinct guides her more than reason. It persuades her to find a way to attract attention and please men without seeming brazen or daring. Such an undertaking requires a happy combination of audacity and reserve, calculation and candor. Only a very real femininity can succeed in this tour de force of awakening a curiosity at once sudden and without distrust, to attract a lively and respectful interest.

Some very rare women are here aided by their charm, this strange thing which is so different from mere physical beauty and which, undefinable though it is, leads us to expect a beautiful nature. This personal radiance always is confined to a small number—and others always distrust them. What a paradox! The women who possess the most charm are, in all other respects, the least arrogant, the least self-assured—which proves that the complexes of weakness and the need for others constitute an integral part of their nature.

Let us not be surprised, then, to see women instinctively looking outside themselves for an ally that will serve their interests without betraying them. They need a silent messenger between themselves and men, one that will present itself without giving warning, be capable of insinuating itself discreetly, and imposing itself without annoying. A messenger which, once brought into play, can be explicit enough to awaken attention and prick curiosity, but enigmatic enough not to spoil the charm of mystery; to make known its origin without betraying its design; to be eloquent enough to arouse favor, but not insistent enough to awaken severe prejudice. To attract and mobilize masculine attention in this way, when so many other things woo this attention and so many delightful distractions menace it, is not easy.

The invisible accomplice will succeed only in the measure that its subtlety matches its delicacy and its tenacity its originality. Lacking these, the thousand whirlwinds that ceaselessly agitate the capricious masculine attention will sweep it away like a straw.

But what except perfume could perform such a task? Gestures and words and even glances are never delicate enough; they are either too timid or too daring. And the most inspired of dress styles, however important, turns away most of the attention of those who notice it by substituting themselves for those who wear them; elegant clothes often betray the cause they pretend to serve.

When all is said and done, perfume is the only ally on which a woman can fully count. It permits her to attract without losing her reserve, to unveil herself while keeping her modesty, to impose herself without importuning, to insist without wearying, and, above all, to express herself without giving away any of her mystery.

Perhaps now we begin to see the reason for the innate attraction, deep as her being itself, of woman to perfume. Perfume is, in her sight, much more than an ornament; it is a true outward projection of her very personality. Hence her needs—and her hesitations—in this domain.

The sharp sense every true woman possesses of her own individuality, her chances of pleasing and of displeasing, prevents her from allowing the caprices of luck to choose "her" perfume. There is nothing she studies or calculates so meticulously; her choice is dependent upon what she knows of herself (and never confides) and of the opportunities of the hour, the light, and the season.

The least fault in this respect has more serious consequences for her than a mistake about a fabric or a color. The perfume a woman wears often allows us to judge her more surely than her bearing or her speech; it shows her taste and, through this, the quality of her deep instinct. Her perfume classifies her.

So genius has always been consulted. Genius has been able to invent varieties of perfume which are almost as numerous and subtle as characters or feelings. There are delicate perfumes, violent ones, noble and vulgar, pure and sensual perfumes, discreet and provocative ones. In the very image of the human heart

> There are perfumes fresh as the flesh of infants,
> Sweet as an oboe, green as prairies;
> And other corrupt, rich and triumphant,
>
> Expanded like infinite things.
> Such are musk, ambergris, benjamin and frankincense,
> Which sing the transports of mind and senses.

Baudelaire did not exaggerate at all here. From the heart that entrusts its message to perfume, to the heart that receives it, the contact established bears the imprint, noble or vulgar, of the chosen perfume.

There are, of course, perfumes and perfumes. One perfume does not entirely fill its role unless it is able to be a woman's faithful and efficient messenger. The admirable thing is that human art can succeed in making perfumes that are marvels of technique and of psychology. There are great perfumes that are living syntheses of unique qualities. In them we find the power of radiation united to lightness, penetration and at the same time delicacy, personality without showiness, a tenacity that is not insistent.

But always, what assures their high quality is the thing

which for want of a better term we call their depth, their power of enveloping. A perfume generates a living atmosphere, with its volume, its currents, its eddies, its vibrations, even its stridencies. It constitutes an invisible mass in the heart of which it works: it unveils one being to another, enough so to present it truly, but not enough to betray it. This combination of precise and vague constitutes the marvelous success, the materialization of the secret dream to which woman aspires: to be at the same time present and unattainable, recognized and hidden. From her, as from a beautiful perfume, comes forth a radiance whose center we can never define.

Perfume proclaims itself the worthy instrument and perfect symbol of the power of weakness and fragility, the subtle, complete revenge of a femininity faithful to itself.[4]

3.

> Oil and perfume rejoice the heart,
> as the sweetness of a friend whose
> counsel comes from love.

This is not a saying from profane literature, but from the Book of Proverbs, the Holy Bible, inspired by God. More than a whole discourse, it helps us understand the real and symbolic uses, which at first seem baffling, that religion makes of perfume. In the Orient, as in the Occident, pagans and Jews had recourse to it in their worship of the

---

[4] In practice, the use of perfume serves ends more vulgar and basely sensual than those here set forth, but this does not alter the essential data of the problem. The perversion of good things cannot force us to forget their proper qualities. The most noble music can also serve ignoble ends. Must we then, whenever we speak of anything, mention possible deviations? There is no lack of documents that tell the whole sad story.

living and the dead. We shall speak of its use in Christianity.

In the Old Testament, perfumes played a triple part—in anointings, in worship, and in teaching. In the instructions Moses repeated to his people, God decreed that consecrated men should be anointed with an especially perfumed oil. So they were marked, and their status sealed by the indelible infusion of the oil, their prestige evoked by the blessed perfume.

Perfume was also used in worship. The altar of incense was next to the altar of sacrifice. The offering of incense was a great rite, more noble and delicate than that of bloody victims. By its grace and lightness it marvelously evoked the ascending to God of the best act of human beings—their prayers.

To man praying to God or God accepting the prayer, Holy Scripture offers many analogies with perfume. As far as man is concerned, the very invisibility of the fragrance suggests the spirituality of the soul's acts; we recall that, in prayer, the heart is at its purest and least material, and the ascending power of the sweet waves symbolizes this mounting up toward God. Of the perfume itself, as it gushes so mysteriously out of the core of a substance or a plant, and sings like a cricket and shrinks on the coals, it seems to represent the very cause of its outburst in the hidden heart: filial trust.

On God's side, the image of perfume takes on a still more moving significance. With a calm daring, inspired by the Lord, the Holy Book does not fear to say that God gives prayer a welcome very like the welcome we naturally give to perfume. For what is more cordially and joyfully received than a beautiful scent? No one remains passive in its presence. It catches him, strikes him, draws him from his indifference or distraction; it summons him, engrosses him, makes him good-humored in spite of himself. So God reacts before a heart in prayer; He is captivated. He joins Himself with this prayer and waits, as if to savor it and penetrate its secret. Its hold on Him is real and mysterious. Like a beautiful perfume, whose sweet power succeeds in making us forget bad odors, prayer has the astonishing power of distracting God from the unfavorable impression made by our wretchedness and our faults, to make Him interested only in our good will, our praise and confidence, our repentance. So, physical though it is, the inexplicable but undeniable success of a lovely perfume on those who breathe it in contains a spiritually moving lesson. There is nothing arbitrary about it; God has not disdained to show Himself to us breathing in and rejoicing at the odor of prayers and the sight of His just ones!

The radiation of perfume, Biblical symbol of personal communication of the soul with God, is also the symbol of the social bonds that God wishes to prevail among His children.

As used in public worship, perfume scattered or burnt symbolizes the spiritual unity of those it envelops. It reminds them that their community ought to be as agreeable to frequent as the scented air is to breathe. It is an invitation to make those feelings and acts into something as delicate and delicious as the multifold elements of which perfume is composed; so the community will be like the fragrant mists rising toward God.

As though to sanctify and bless it anew, Christ has Himself explicitly taken up the image again. To grieving minds and stern wills, He recalls that virtue never dispenses from good grace and that charity must, above all, remain kindly. Neither sacrifice nor faith goes with morose sadness. "As for you, when you fast, anoint your heads. . . ." On the lips of the Saviour, perfume becomes a concrete reminder of the attractiveness and graciousness, comeliness and tact from which a Christian should never deviate.

When one speaks of Christ in the same breath with such a topic as perfume, one does so deliberately—and advisedly. By the words of the Apostle St. Paul, He is the Anointed One par excellence—that is, the One penetrated and impregnated with marvelously perfumed Grace, in which is concentrated to the highest degree the opulence and the attraction of the exquisite perfume of God.

By this astonishing and audacious analogy, borrowed from the Psalms, St. Paul suggests to us the ineffable compenetration of humanity by Divinity, in which the very mystery of the Being of the Word Incarnate consists.[5]

The best thing is that these expressions, drawn from so humble a reality, are so faithful to the great Reality they evoke. They should help us better to grasp the infinite richness of Christ, inexhaustible source of the very treasures of

---

[5] Of such teaching St. Thomas Aquinas notes that the name of "Christ" (anointed) is the one which expresses the hypostatic union: "*Christus, in quo intelligitur, et divinitas ungens, et humanitas uncta.*"

God, the great but invisible radiance of the Word made flesh, the hearth of all light and all spiritual warmth among us. But above all they show Him to us in the overwhelming attraction of His wonderful lovableness. So the Pauline image of perfumed anointing joins with and emphasizes that of the Canticle of Canticles. In all purity and in perfect fullness, the magnificent texts celebrating the charm of perfumes of the beloved symbolize the secret of the ardor of Christians toward their God.

So we can conceive that, since then, the Apostle St. Paul has made "the good odor of Jesus Christ" the word of command for the faithful, the very exemplar of their activity in this world!

The Gospel does not supply them with any of the advantages of warlike force, any of the carnal means on which most of humanity's leaders base their influence. But they need not regret that. They have something infinitely better: they possess a power efficient and penetrating in another way—charity, which, in the spiritual order, is the living replica of perfume. The triumphs of perfume, imponderable but so deep, aid the faithful to understand better the exact sense and true import of God's promises: "Fear not, little flock: I have overcome the world." In proving to us that there are other ways to succeed than by using brute force, perfume contributes to the defense of the primacy of spiritual values.

Faithful to the lessons of the Bible and to the example of Christ, the Church has integrated perfume into her liturgy under the form of incensing at the beginning, and throughout the course of solemn ceremonies—thus providing for the senses a symbolic representation of the invisible action that is taking place.

She assigns perfume a part in her most profound rites. She has deliberately decreed that the oil used in certain sacraments must be perfumed, under pain of nullity. It seems to her essential that to the symbolism of oil, representing the strength conferred by grace, should be added the symbolism of "good odor." For it is fitting that there should be evoked at the same time the reality of the anointing of Christ and the "diffusion of grace," the first effect of sacramental action.

Anyone can understand a language so simple. By comparison with the welcome we reserve for a lovely perfume, our contacts with God show forth in their gravity. The divine action penetrates to our most secret thoughts and desires. As efficaciously and intimately as perfume acts on our emotions, the divine life, when we accept it, penetrates through all our thoughts and our desires. Moreover, the diffusion of a good odor permits St. Paul to interpret unequivocally the demands of Christ's love: Charity. The action which it performs requires strength, but also delicacy; personality, but allied to good taste; tenacity, but also gentle grace.

So perfume reminds us and shows us that influence, even physical influence, is not necessarily dependent on material volume. The subtlety of its action makes us put our finger, as it were, on the relative unimportance of brute material power. What use is a power that cannot find the road to our hearts? Impalpable and fragile perfume discovers this road. So it has an important place in our lives. Yes, it can trouble the sensibilities and cast a spell over hearts, but it can also open the mind to much higher realities. That is why, though one can curse and scorn it, no one can disregard it. It is a power we must reckon with.

Second Part

❖

DIRECT CONTACT

❖

❖

❖

❖

❖

CHAPTER I

Touch: The Sense of Presence and Contact

1.

THE WORLD of brute creation is made up of solid objects whose lineaments, fixed and congealed, remain impenetrable. The skin of a living being endowed with sensation is not impermeable in this way. Its more fragile and supple texture shows us that we have another kind of body here. Even though all things belong to the order of quantities possessing weight and mass, and existing in space and time, animated matter is a sharply original kind of substance. Its physical quantity is sublimated, organized for ends superior to those of inert matter. Its greater delicacy is the mark of its aptitude to enter into relations and exchanges with others; when sensitivity is added, we leap the abyss that separates the order of brute quantity, where meetings are nothing but juxtapositions, from the order of living organisms, where contacts are *presences*.

Touch is the first manifestation of this sensitivity of living beings to realities outside themselves; and touch is defined in general as the permeability of our physical periphery. While things go on inside, physical pressures exerted on us are transferred by touch into divers sensations that allow us to know about the things that touch us or happen to us.

Touch is different from all other senses; it is not localized in an organ. It uses myriads of nerves joined to papillae that are distributed on all parts of the skin. This astonishing extension is not vague or inexact. It is a true projection of signals, as many as they are varied, covering the entire body, and always in action.

It is a strange thing that this immense and valuable labor eludes our conscious activity. We see practically nothing of the way these innumerable branches function and how intensely they vibrate. Whether we are asleep or awake, they continue working, setting off instinctive reactions not under the control of the will. Whether we wish it or not, they impose on us impressions resulting from our state in fact—our situation—and with such objectivity that we think the contacts of touch are the very model of evidence and certitude.[1]

Crude as this sometimes seems, the awakening to external realities is far from simple. The sensations of touch are more complex and rich than their vague name would at first lead us to think. They are as varied as the kind of pressures that physical realities can exert. This is why the

---

[1] *Translator's note:* We remember that the Apostle Thomas insisted on touching with his hand before he would believe.

divers reactions they awaken constitute so many co-ordi-
nates used by the brain in its spontaneous activity to draw
the maximum benefit—or to avoid as much inconvenience
as possible—from the environment. So touch plays the
often-unwelcome part of warning and advising the vital
instinct. Learning from these experiences, we impose on
our actions a more prudent and more skillful discipline, pre-
served from the illusions and pretensions of the a priori.
Once we have come up against the toughness of reality we
no longer act with the insolence of a demigod. In initiating
us into the exterior world, touch teaches us, if not to behave like wise men in it, at least not to be victimized by it.

2.

The first kind of evidence the sensation of contact ob-
tains has to do with the physical solidity of bodies. It cannot be doubted that these bodies have actual mass, hard or
soft, great or small, tall or short. The existence of other
things imposes itself upon us, sometimes shocking or
wounding, but incontestable. Near or far, light or oppress-
ing, their presence is nonetheless situated beyond frontiers
we cannot leap, irreducible: they are themselves, and I am
myself.

The abutment upon another, painful or not, which touch
makes us aware of, is also transformed into a perception of
immediate consequences. Rudimentary, it is nevertheless
enough to force the ego out of its prison, to allow the interior vision to surpass its carnal limits, to record different
universes, and to judge them in their solid mass and positive volume. Later, in the course of intellectual temptations
that confront the pretentious ego, the primitive sensation

of direct contact will be the best guardian of good sense, as far as respect for the nature and worth of reality are concerned; there are cases, in fact, where a rock falling on a toe can restore health to a mind better than an eloquent discourse.

Touch not only records the concrete positivity of objects; by feeling them, it can take a real inventory on the spot. Gropingly, like a blind man, it explores surfaces, feels reliefs and patterns, the sinuosity or regularity of ridges, the roughness or polish of materials. Of the results of this prospecting, deaf-mutes furnish us affecting testimony: they are the living proof of the resources of touch. And there are actually professions that base their expertness on the sense of touch: such specialists as judge the genuineness of pearls or the quality of materials by feeling them.

There is no better proof of the value attached to evaluations founded on direct contact than in the very evolution of the idea of "tact." [2] In the intellectual and moral order, tact means the right and fitting reserve in the gestures and words we use to another. The delicacy and subtlety touch can attain have made it the symbol of the most valuable social qualities that rule over human contacts: this indescribable mixture of exactness and emphasis, of delicacy and correctness.[3]

In a less striking sense, but no less useful, touch lets us gain impressions of the temperature of the medium in

[2] *Translator's note:* "Tact" in French means both *tact* and *touch.*
[3] *Translator's note:* If we are tactful, we feel our way in dealing with people.

which we revolve and of the things approaching us. Sensitivity to warmth and cold is one of the most valuable aids in the body's system of self-defense. It sets off the needed reactions, and rules over the changes of rhythm which life needs.

Under the attack of cold, tissues contract and use more calories. Impressions of heat, on the other hand, bring into play a whole system of relaxation, thanks to which the countless cells all open and cleanse themselves. So the human body owes to touch the power of living under atmospheric differences with a skill of adaptation which is wiser and more lasting than a brute insolence in which the resources of the organism would soon be exhausted. Without any effort on our part, the sensations of heat and cold, sometimes overwhelming and often annoying, have the happy effect of putting us in tune with the great rhythm presiding over our equilibrium and guarantees the duration of beings and of things—the alternation of effort and relaxation, of toil and rest. To appreciate this sense of temperature at its true worth it is enough to notice how sickly bodies become when the progress of civilization allows them to escape the vicissitudes of the seasons. There are many maladies unknown to people who are directly exposed to the rigors of excessive temperatures but which find a chosen terrain in those too strictly sheltered.

The sense of pain, which arises from touch, is still less understood than that of heat and cold. We feel especially the painful side of the lugubrious privilege of suffering. But from the biological point of view this anguish is the nega-

tive aspect of an advantage: in warning us of the noxious-
ness of the realities striking us it lets us react to them in
time. If the first contact with a sharp edge did not hurt us,
how could we avoid being wounded? If the first sensation
of burning did not warn us, how could we help being
burnt? We would not have the recoil that avoids injury.
Painful symptoms give us warning of organic disturbances;
and where symptoms are painless, the disease continues un-
checked and completes incurable ravages.

Truly, the sense of pain is the warning, annoying no
doubt but nevertheless highly valuable, of risks to which
the frailty of our organism exposes us. The inconveniences
it causes us are compensated for by the services it renders.
Although it brings many miseries with it, it always acts as
an excellent guardian of the instinct of self-preservation.

We should mention, at least in passing, the psychological
and moral contributions of pain. The misery it represents
often deepens our thoughts and feelings, and teaches us
indulgence and pity. Without it, how could we ever learn
sympathy and brotherly compassion?

Fortunately, contacts with exterior things are not all
disagreeable, and there is no need to appeal to reason to
justify them. The sense of touch is also the sense of pleasure. In this capacity it occupies a chosen place in the
thoughts of men. Most people, it is true, know only its
delightful aspect. To them it is a source of easy enjoyment,
as intense as it is immediate. That is why they have made
carnal joy in all its forms the chief end of most of their
actions. It alone, and not the context in which it arises,
interests them. They forget that enjoyment demands exact

conditions: skin-deep though it is, pleasure is not born automatically out of every kind of contact. It does not depend upon arbitrary caprice, but is the result of a very objective physical harmony whose precise mission is to signal to the vital instinct. To want to obtain it no matter how, in season and out of season, ends only in deception. By its very structure, physical enjoyment is not an end in itself: its whole destiny is the regulation of life.

It has a duty to point out to consciousness that the reality with which this or that zone of the body enters into contact is favorable to it. Unlike pain, which marks the presence of danger, pleasure marks the presence of something which, objectively, responds to the attention of the subject; so it releases a quite different reaction. Under the assault of suffering, the organism draws back and shuts itself up; pleasure, on the contrary, reassures and stimulates it. The emotion felt is a guidepost and excitant for the vital attention; it makes the attention pause on the subject that arouses it, and incites it to devote more concern to it.

With an objectivity and comprehension to which most so-called "spiritual" people have not accustomed us, St. Thomas Aquinas was pleased to emphasize the usefulness of physical enjoyment. To the most laborious and most necessary functions are attached the most exquisite sensations. In this admirable association, the great theologian sees the imprint of a Wisdom as adroit as it is paternal; by joining pleasure to toil, this Wisdom has made the very effort the immediate cause of its own recompense. It is in the course of its work that the hand experiences the keenest joys, and it is when deeply and properly experiencing them that men can know all the intensity of the joys concerning the reproductive function, the most intimate of all acts and the one most weighted with consequences.

In this tempestuous and delicate domain we must first of all see the original order of things, as God instituted it. So St. Thomas proceeds; and he has given us a more wholesome and profound vision of the carnal joys than all those who exalt the flesh have ever been able to contrive.

The serious and exacting duty of the transmission of life is united with a power of extreme enjoyment, and the marvelous thing about it is that the whole body enters into it. The difference in physical construction which permits the dividing and sharing of these duties also creates a reciprocity that transforms the exchanges between man and woman into bonds that are necessarily complementary. Even to its least details, their faculty of enjoyment is so arranged and adapted to their differences of structure that they must be attuned to one another; and this teaches them their mutual dependence.

Without the crowning touch of pleasure, these acts would lose their human sense. They would have only a physical utility; the contact would not be fervent, desire would be only a need, and satisfaction only a vulgar satiation. Because it is made to be reciprocal, sexual enjoyment consummates and magnifies the mutual attraction of man and woman. It enables them not only to endure, but even to love, their differences. Thanks to it, their meeting is not purely instinctive; the two hearts beat as one, their contact is transformed into union and their embrace into mutual revelation. So much so that, in the absence of this joy, sexual activity becomes simply a function; nervous expenditure shows its brutality, relaxation is only fatigue, and the consequences arising from it are an intolerable burden.

Indeed, the reciprocity of pleasure in two bodies that unite is one of the essential conditions of the fullness of their fusion. On an inferior plane, no doubt—but an important one!—it shows concretely the aspirations of the most exalted and pure aspects of human love: the forgetting of self, and the solicitude for another. So the Creator has willed, He the first author of the constitution of man and woman. Instead of being almost a deification of the flesh, this reciprocity of influence in the awakening and accomplishing of sexual pleasure implies an invitation to a truer love, for it cannot be achieved unless there is a struggle against egotism. The success of this communality of joy requires conditions which the violence of pure desire cannot know how to fulfill.

By a strange sort of paradox, which Manicheanism and many severe moralists doubt, but which elementary psychology reveals, care for the pleasure of another ennobles desire and makes it holy. This requires a self-mastery, a patience, a delicacy that come from something higher than the glands. It presupposes a love of the person of the loved one, strong enough to impose on our own body a restraint of haste and violence. In this domain where instinctive avidity seems to rule, forethought for the joy of another obliges us to be generous, even a little ascetic!

It is not the Creator's fault if, by their egotism and perversity, men have corrupted the sense of physical enjoyment. Isolating it from its context, they have made sexual pleasure something as violent as it is lamentable, as deceptive as it is sterile, where restraints do not count: something just good enough to serve as matter for statistics. God did not link deception to life! Whatever use human beings may make of the body, the sense of touch is there, and its very structure bears witness that the Creator has neglected nothing to make the most carnal relations enlightened and exalted by joy.

While it is not localized in a particular organ, the sense of touch has its own precise physiological elements. From the periphery of the body to the medullary and brain centers, the science of anatomy discovers and follows nerve fibers specializing in palpation, in temperature, in pain, in pleasure. We know the course of direct touch, immediate pressure.

There is another and more subtle form of touch; facts compel us to admit its existence without allowing us to analyze it. It consists in the influence of certain waves which do not work by direct contact. Besides and in the margin of clear perceptions there exists a whole range of more diffuse discernments upon which, more than upon those of fixed sensation and discursive reason, presentiment and intuition feed. They are brought to bear on some of the most subtle offerings of the physical universe—those strange effluvia of persons and of things which are the most intimate individual radiation of concrete presences. We have a striking confirmation of this indefinable aura emanating from living persons, in the consciousness love has of it. People who love one another often discern from incredible distances the state and movements of their dear one. And if the artist were not psychically in tune with reality, he could not perceive it so intensely.

Truly, we find ourselves here in the presence of an aptitude of the human body in which all elements of the body concur; but touch seems to dominate. It seems that it is a question of sensitivity to the most delicate vibrations of the body. Some people, less and less numerous of late, would smile at extrasensory perception and other attempts at detection which are strange to the methods and practices of ordinary scientific experimentation. They forget that physical reality contains more richness and complexity than our five senses can record. Fifty years ago, nobody would have dared to predict the variety of waves which we now know the least bit of reality sends out. So much progress has been made in detecting and recording waves by means of apparatus made from inert matter that we may well pause to reflect on the potentialities of the apparatus we call the human body, which is wonderful in its own special way. Who can define a priori the limits of its receptive resources?

At a time when people were ignorant of almost all the world of waves and the marvels of physics, St. Thomas Aquinas had already stated that the universe and the human body both held many surprises. Against those who wanted to limit what was then known of the human body into definitive formulae, founded upon experimentation that was accurate but brief, he declared that we should

judge its possibilities, not according to its biological construction, but according to the virtues of the mind animat-
ing and elevating it. This is a very far-reaching principle!
And how wise in its daring, for it takes into account the
perfections that future progress can bring.

Not without humor, St. Thomas advises us not to shut
ourselves up in our own little personal evidences, and not
to refuse, in their name, the inventions and conclusions of
others under the pretext that they come into collision with
our mental habits, even our scientific ones! Like all human
things, the most rational discoveries are first presented as
hypotheses and intuitions, which often have no other support than obscure presentiments and feelings. A fine thing!
A greater sensitivity, which explores new roads, is not
necessarily foolish; quite the contrary. "Of all the animals,"
St. Thomas said, "man possesses the most perfect touch
(because of the delicacy of his organism). And among men
themselves, those whose touch is the most subtle are also
the most intelligent. This is shown by the fact that we
consider those whose flesh is the most delicate as intel-
lectually the best endowed." (*"Et inter homines ipsos, qui
sunt melioris tactus, sunt melioris intellectus. Cujus signum
est quod molles carne bene aptos mente videmus."*)

From its origin and through the whole course of intellectual and moral activity, *perceptibilitas*—that is, sensory
contact with reality—is of first importance. Not only because it is the common documentary instrument, but also
because it is the helper whose quality conditions even the
use of spiritual activities. This text from the great theo-

logian says a great deal for his sense of human unity. There is nothing he reproves so much as a "spirituality" that insists on dissociating immaterial from carnal activities. To him, the cohesion of body and soul is so profound in us that the perfection of one conditions that of the other. Realism can be carried no further.

Our interior world, which nourishes mind and heart, depends upon our contacts with realities, and primarily upon touch which perceives presences. Underneath their still rudimentary exteriors, touch procures for us the feeling of solid actuality, its resistance, and, in part, its value. Thanks to it, we know at last the nuisance value or the true benefit of the things we meet. Onto these fundamental data, useful or noxious, of reality, are grafted all the others.

Hence the importance of touch. When heavy and gross, it perceives only the most brutal of contacts; the details of reality escape it—the most gifted mind could not divine them under such conditions. When touch is delicate and subtle, it detects nuances and opens the intelligence to the thousand trifles without which there is no minute knowledge.

Without tact that is active and precise and highly impressionable, however exact and lucid intellectual grasp may be, it always lacks something of that delicacy and facility by which we recognize the fineness of the mind.

❖

CHAPTER II

The Hand

1.

IT IS not always apparent how fundamentally unique the human body is. Its physiochemical components and biological and sensory reactions can scarcely be distinguished from those of animals. The radiance of the spirit often remains concealed. But still there is an organ whose morphology and activity at first sight betray the presence of the soul: the hand.

The physiology of the hand is purely carnal, but its behavior shows the imprint of a force sprung from something higher, reveals something of a free personality. This is so true that, spontaneously, neither ignorant people nor scholars treat it as a commonplace organ. While of other parts of the body, even the most precious, we say only that they are what they are or that they do what they can, we hold the hand responsible for its acts. We demand an accounting from it. Of all our members, it is the only one we feel we must describe in moral language, exactly the same language of praise or blame that we use for the conscious personality. We judge the hand, and proclaim it industrious or lazy, courageous or cowardly, generous or grasping, bene-factor or criminal.

What is the basis for such exceptional treatment?

We say "the hand" although there are two: the right and the left. But they work so well together, and comple-ment each other so adequately, that they are practically one. So we have formed the habit of treating them as a unique unity. They are so constructed that they can work together as well as independently of each other.

Their very structure earns them this independence. Everything about them is planned for mobility and flexi-bility. But at the price of a great complexity! Artful and protected as it is, we cannot help feeling something of the extraordinary character of this organism. Even the articula-tion of the wrist, attaching the hand to the forearm as it does, while separating it from the forearm's rigidity, im-plies a co-ordination even more delicate than that of the most perfected machines.

On this movable pivot are hung the first articulations of the fingers—but the word "hung" cannot be right, since each bony joint adheres without coercion. Branching off from the palm, the visible separation of the fingers takes place, and the fingers themselves are divided into movable phalanges. On one side, the thumb, larger and stronger, is opposed to the four others, which are parallel but inde-pendent.

In this very opposition of the thumb and the fingers lies the essential condition of the hand's usefulness. To this fact the hand owes its prehension, which means that it is capable not only of reaching and touching, but even, and especially, grasping and holding. Without this opposition of the thumb, the articulations of the hand might permit it to envelop and even somewhat to shape objects, but not to fasten upon them and take hold of them, grasp and lift them.

The consequences of this fundamental power are incalculable. Each one of the hands being endowed with it, work on things is made possible; grasping does not exhaust the possibilities of contact. Master of this power, in the presence of what he holds, man can remain himself and exercise his action. If he did not take advantage of the facility and the extreme mobility of the hand, the most refined genius would act like a common animal; without the hand, there could be no elegance, even in eating. In enabling us to carry food to our mouths, it frees us from the obligation of bending over a trough!

What does the weakness of the hands matter? Their skill assures them triumphs even more formidable than those of muscles and claws and fangs. Their strength always remains controlled and delicate. To keep what it holds, the hand does not need to crush it. And its very delicacy keeps it from acting brutally: it would be the first victim to suffer from its violence, for it has feelings. In the very organ of skill and strength resides one of the most impressionable centers of touch. The same fingers that can accomplish so many things, and can squeeze so strongly, capture the most subtle vibrations and know the secret of the sweetest caresses.

Is there any domain in which the hand does not have a part to play? We find it used everywhere. This evidence is confirmed by observation, but its secret is by no means explained. That a simple carnal organ can so well translate and execute the least decisions of the mind implies a co-ordination that is itself a mystery.

We know, of course, about the anatomical installation that ties this mixture of bone and flesh, nerves and muscles, veins and tendons, to the brain, the seat of conscious activity. We know the details of the network through which the current passes. But we can arrive at no explanation of the strange solidarity prevailing between the hand and the personality. With unheard-of promptness and self-effacement, the hand obeys the slightest impulse of the will. Whatever it may cost it, the hand performs the most difficult gestures and actions and works without the least dispute about it. And, in compensation, it enjoys a privilege unknown (at least in the same degree) to other organs: it *develops*. The hand can be educated, as well as the mind.

A discreet servant, the hand works completely unmindful of itself. Yet it bears traces of our works. Its features are modified in the course of the years. The uses to which we put it make it more sensitive or tough, strengthen or weaken it. It participates so closely in our battles and our intimate duties that finally it bears a reflection of our history.

Painters and sculptors treat the hands as "a second face of the soul." Their shape and behavior, their nobility or vulgarity, their fineness and their utility, their calm and their nervousness announce, at least in some degree, our qualities of character and heart. "Show me your hands, and

I will tell you, if not with certitude, at least with some reason, what you are."

Without pretending to the subtleties (or the doubtful claims) of chirology, common sense judges the worth of a man by the use he makes of his hands. The quantity and quality of work accomplished are a merciless criterion of courage and real talent. Just as "we know the tree by its fruits," so we gauge a personality by its concrete works. The positive accomplishments of life rest in our hands, for they are the instruments of human efficacy.

In our social relations, the use we make of the hand is extremely revealing. Incarnate spirits, we depend on the hand to express our thoughts and feelings. Our most sincere promises seem to lack seriousness if we do not give our hands on them.

Love and friendship, comradeship and business relations each have their own gestures. The thousand ways of shaking hands or of saluting make up a language as subtle as that of words. In spite of ourselves, our handshakes reveal us. Their spontaneity or reticence, firmness or limpness are indications of what we contain within ourselves.

Nor can we neglect to point out the "indiscreet" character of writing, the direct work of the hand that writes. Certainly the fingers obey the dictates of the mind, but through their movements passes something of the vitality and the rhythm of the temperament. Just as every work made by a tool bears the mark of the tool, so in writing lie the traits of the living context the hand sets down.

In all domains the hands work; not as a tool whose skill is its only worth, but as companions and associates sharing the best and the worst, the pain and the success. We entrust everything to them; our labor and our skill, our affections and our thoughts. They carry out our least desires with an admirable disinterestedness. Their destiny is inextricably mingled with our own. Alas, they are equally at the mercy of our perverse wishes, and, at the same time, their story includes disappointments and cruel chapters. It is enough to mention them; they bear witness to the dreadful consequences of this manual power when the heart uses it badly. Thank God, it is not always thus; for the hand, in itself, is a gift so sublime that the Lord Himself has reserved a chosen place for it in His revelations.

2.

Many times over, and with serene assurance, the Bible speaks of the hand of God. Not in a literal sense, of course; God, having no body, cannot possess a physical hand. What light, nonetheless, does such a symbol cast upon the role of the Creator and on His relations with His works! The great Rodin, in his genius, felt this, and of "The Hand of God" made one of his noblest masterpieces. He sculptured it, marvelously strong and delicate, lovingly shaping a formless block from which emerge two bodies. In viewing this unforgettable statue, we hear a most pure echo of the inspired Book.

The Bible sees the hand of the Creator as the true expression of His sovereign power and of the personal touch of His activity. He produces and shapes His works directly: with a holy jealousy, He takes upon Himself the invention and the planning, the making and shaping of all things. He keeps for Himself the paternity of creation, and He reveals His role as Creator through human words strictly reserved for manual action and implying immediate contact, such as "make, shape, fashion, touch, form."

This same hand sustains and guides the world it has created. It shelters and protects the most humble of the beings born of His love. Everything, from the weakest blade of grass to the greatest angel, is "in the hands of God." Unlike ours, the divine hands do not know inconstancy or weakness; an infinite tenderness always inspires them. To persuade us of this, God confided to His prophet these words in which the most obscure workman can feel something of his own attachment to all that has required effort of him: "Behold, I have graven thee in My hands" (Isa. 49:16).

Christ took up and applied to its fullest extent the immense, disturbing lesson contained in this symbolism when He said, "My Father works." God at labor—God, like a good and skillful workman, putting into His work the best of Himself.

God has done even more. Since the Incarnation, His hand is no longer a symbol but a reality. The Word made flesh has made it the instrument of His personal activity.

Christ has lived the whole history of the human hand. He has known all its awkwardness and all its possibilities. He educated and disciplined His baby hands. His adult hands were the instruments of His livelihood, before they began to distribute the miracles of His grace. Thanks to them, His most divine activity assumes a manifestation that alone can touch and reassure us: the very movements of familiar contact.

When all was consummated, the work of obedience completed, His very last word was to give His soul back "into the hands of His Father." For His own hands that had done so much, He reserved a chosen place in His supreme sacrifice. In the terrible repose of death, nailed to the cross, open forever, they continued their mission. From them until the end of time, blood flows upon the world, and with it, compassion and pardon.

The Church has treasured this message. Following the Apostles, the first depositories of the thought of Christ, the Church sees in the laying on of hands the sacramental rite par excellence. On ordination day the consecrating power flows from the consecrated hands of the bishop, in whom resides the fullness of authority. In the name of Christ, he extends his hands over the future deacons and future priests. Then, completing this more remote gesture by immediate contact, the bishop, with his own hands, anoints the palms and the fingers of those being ordained.

So down the centuries the action of Christ continues to be exercised through human hands. Without the assurance of His help, what priest would dare claim to consecrate, to pardon, to console? Such interventions surpass the power of man. Not without emotion, the priest, before consecrating the Body and the Blood of his God, twice evokes the memory of those "holy and venerable hands." And this at the most sublime moment of the exercise of his priestly power.

They tell us everything, those hands!—sovereign power and infinite goodness and the grandeur of the humility of the tremendous Personality who knows the most humble details of our humanity. Their daily remembrance assures us that the prodigious overture still endures; through and by means of the consecrated hands of His priests, Christ comes and abides, with all that He is and with all that He has.

This spiritual interpretation will have a great deal to do with the value we place on the work of the hands. Christianity was the first panegyrist of the basic nobility of manual labor. Against the great Plato, who appreciated only mental work, stands the Church: it cannot permit such snobbery; the very example of God forbids.

The Gospel but confirms this emphasis on the importance of the hand. On the lips of Christ, "to do" is the necessary complement of "to love." Positive actions and effective materializations alone count in the sight of God. With idle hands, the most beautiful ideal is only an illusion, and the most ardent charity a useless sentiment. Indeed, human hands have always found their most noble and most exacting inspiration in charity.

We should not be surprised at this. Everyday life proves clearly that, if it is to give its best, the hand requires, not the intensity of selfish or vile passions, but the awakening of the best things in our hearts.

Without maternal love, would a woman's hands have the tenacity and courage required of them? To this immense love, woman's hands owe their gentleness and their patience, their courage and their devotion. Without them the finest heart would be powerless.

"It takes twenty years to make a man," sings Péguy. Who would dare to count the works of a mother's hands? They prepared a cradle for the new-born child; they received the child, fed it, changed it, rocked it, soothed it. Later they guided the child's steps, dressed its wounds, dried its tears; they distracted and consoled it, educated and corrected it. And all the while they were taking care of a thousand material details: cooking, washing, ironing, sewing, mending.

Not for an instant do they stop, these hands. If for one day their labor is interrupted, then pain, anguish, disarray, and disorder are on the threshold! Everything depends on them, so valiant, so gentle. But who takes count of this and renders homage to them? The love that inspires them is so silent and discreet. How many sons, alas! have for the first time realized their existence when they are seen quiet in death, motionless forever.

Mystery of the maternal heart! Except for the death of a child, there is no worse suffering for it than the conviction of uselessness. Of all agonies, not to have anyone to help, protect, console, and care for is the most intolerable.

Maternal hands do not fulfill their wonderful office in peace unless others can protect and support them: the working hands of a man.

These hands are the proper artisans of their labor, and often the victims. The risks here are numerous, and wear and tear almost inevitable. They must, in order to keep on, have higher reasons than their own interest alone: the love of a profession, and, above all, the courage of a man who is determined to confront life. With his own hands, the worker acquires infinitely more than his salary: the legitimate pride of owing to no one but himself the bread that he and his family have to eat. So Chesterton could write: "It is no more shameful for a muddy man to be soiled than for a sponge-fisher to be wet. A chimney-sweep covered with soot is no more dishonored than Michelangelo covered with clay or Bayard covered with blood."

When circumstances lend themselves to it, the hands become the instruments of personal skill and the creative sense, besides being the means of earning a living. They enable the workman to realize the profound desire that every man conscious of his power carries in his own heart —to work according to his own ideas, to stamp his work with his own truly personal imprint.

It does not matter what the exact nature of his work is. The difference between the artisan who loves a work well done and the artist mindful of beauty is not very great; each one has the noble ambition of imposing his own will on brute matter. Artisans and artists cannot be separated. Against this distinction, Rodin, in the name of his own manual experiences and the love of his medium, exploded with, "For more than a century people have separated what they call 'great art' from 'crafts.' As if art were not a great ensemble of them all!" [1]

The problems to be solved and their solutions are, in

---

[1] A formula of Louis Nizier well expresses the communality and the difference of the forms of manual activity: "He who works with his hands is a workman; he who uses his hands and his brain is an artisan; but the man who works with his hands, his brain, and his heart is an artist."

both cases, absolutely the same: collusion of the creative spirit with inert matter; conflict between the wish for initiative and originality on the one hand, and, on the other hand, the recalcitrance or weakness of the materials. If the hand did not determine by direct contact the quality and the real possibilities of what is given it, the desires of talent —even talent amounting to genius—would run grave danger of miscarrying. Before these desires can be realized, the hand must preside over the adaptation of the mind to the concrete conditions of reality.

Thus the humble hand of the artisan regulates the work. Long experience with work has always rightly considered that a respect for the information brought by the hand is an essential factor in forming the mind. "To take it in hand" implies a progress in judgment and reflection. So real workers are wise. In the course of constant touching with their hands they have discovered the heart of a secret that books do not teach: the secret of the irreplaceable character of manual contact and of the slow and persistent education of the sense of touch. Whether it is a question of a totally utilitarian work or of a great masterpiece, success implies manual skill as much as ideas. Delacroix said of Puget:

> He began by being a workman; that is the best education a man can receive for those arts where the hand is the tool (and are there any others?); it results in a practice and a patience in the execution of details which a man cannot learn in an academy.

Without the craftsman's hand, genius would remain sterile.

3.

"Instrument of instruments," the hand has the astonishing power of adapting itself precisely to the kind of service we demand of it; the range of its applications would require almost as huge an account book as that of the mind. So we find it at the very center of the most subtle of all arts in the world—music.

In its essence, the universe of sounds, unlike that of solid matter, is at the entire mercy of the musician who produces it. He is absolute master of their combinations and rhythms. And yet, left to itself, the most gifted inspiration would not be enough to assure the existence of the masterpieces it creates. If writing did not fix and preserve it, all music would vanish as soon as it was born. The most sublime inspiration needs a hand to transcribe it. To succeed in doing this, the hand must be educated, accustomed to signs, synchronized—or almost so—to the external cadence. Under these conditions it gives body to music.

But this is still only an imperfect incarnation. "A musical score is only a *promise* of music," said Keyserling. Music does not assume its true form until it has been transferred into sounds. Then, taking wings, it becomes really and fully itself. What gives it life? To a certain extent, the human voice can set it free. But the voice cannot present complex works which are beyond its own simplicity. To whom can we entrust them, then, if not to the hand? It alone can animate the multiple instruments of sound which, under the direction of the inventive mind, its own skill has brought into being. If it did not go through hands and literally come out from the fingertips of the artist, music, properly so called, could not exist at all.

We behold here one of the most extraordinary revelations of the resources of the human hand. Musical execution demands that the skill of the workman be developed to virtuosity. The muscular and nervous reflexes have to be capable of adapting themselves, with minute fidelity and deceptive velocity, to the most difficult combinations. To tell the truth, all hands are not capable of this education. It requires basic organic dispositions that can be developed but not acquired; such include supple wrists, clever fingers, quick reactions. Work, laborious work, must be added to them. Of all the arts, music demands the most total and devoted fidelity on the part of the most gifted people. The "sleight of hand" it requires is so delicate and so extremely careful that, if it is not practiced daily, it loses its mastery. "If I cease to work one day," said Paderewski, "I feel it the next day; a week afterward, the critics notice it; two weeks later, the general public is aware of it."

Music exacts a manual facility so perfect that the artist transcends all mechanical management to concentrate his attention on the most precious part of his art: to rediscover, reanimate, re-create the true inspiration of the one he interprets. Has he any doubt that he owes this freedom, this correspondence of soul, this success in translation, to the obedience of his hands? And this obedience is not passive; the hand responds to the slightest movements of the mind, to the faintest pressure of the will. In its own way, and as if on its own account, the hand realizes the most subtle and delicate requests of the musical sense. The rhythm and nuances, the atmosphere of a work, the communion with the soul of the master—all must pass through this humble workman. Great musicians would not be possible if the hand were not susceptible of being literally and fully synchronized to the least vibrations of the deepest emotions of the heart itself. We sometimes admire the grand total of efforts which result in success, but do we ever stop to think of the marvelous alchemy to which all musical art owes its realization?

For it really is a question of alchemy. An inert, cold page, blackened with signs, becomes a living world that acts upon hearts and enchants them. And the hand is the living crucible of this alchemy: in it and through it the signs taken in by the eyes and deciphered by the mind, felt by the heart, translated into nervous influx by the brain, become stamped and weighed, powerful percussions or imperceptible rustlings. The hand relives and incarnates, in the most active and positive sense of the words, what the artist feels in his secret heart.

We do not suspect that this great miracle is taking place. In the course of a musical performance, the hands of the executant seduce us by their exterior play. We admire their ease and their grace, their speed and their skill, but the most moving thing of all escapes us: this union, in the artist's hands, of extraordinary mechanical skill and a refined sensibility, a minute attention and a total self-forgetfulness in the presence of the work of another. Alas, these two magicians know nothing of the grandeur of the act they perform, the miracle they work, the tumultuous passions they transmit. Blind and deaf, they know nothing of all their work—except its fatigue.[2]

[2] Other things being equal, we can say the same of much of the work the hands do in other arts. The matter on which they exercise their action is more tangible and massive, and hides in part the spirituality of the part they play in the work. But fundamentally their role there is just as remarkable.

The love of beauty has drawn wonderful masterpieces from humankind, and the needs of the artistic sense have developed manual skill to an unbelievable degree. The docile hand lends itself to these sublime caprices. But there is a still more moving use of its power, that motivated by the desire to nurse and to heal. The hand is the instrument of the battle against suffering, the aide of the genius for healing.

Without the hand, how could we ever understand what healing is? Practicing physicians in all times have appreciated its indispensable help. So those who have devoted themselves to the art of healing have always chosen to be called by a name that is really a tribute to the hand: surgeons.[3]

A surgeon's hand is not the hand of an ordinary workman. It involves a difficult and varied context of knowledge, experience, and intelligence. It must possess a skill as great in its own field as the artist's skill. Its action can be neither facile nor improvised. It must keep a strict watch over itself every instant, for upon its discipline, its sureness, its technique, depends the issue of a battle just as difficult as the war waged by the artist against the difficulties of a composition. And the battle is over life and death. That is why the surgeon's hand, as much as his knowledge, is the incarnation both of his personal integrity and of his sense of the seriousness of his mission.

[3] *Translator's note:* Surgeon: from ME surgien, old French cirurgien, sururgien, from cirurgie, sirurgie; from LL chirurgia (surgery).
Chirurgeon: obsolete English for surgeon, from Latin chirurgus, Greek cheirourgos, a surgeon; from cheir (hand) and ergos (work).

The hands of the physician are not slaves for all that. We expect more of the surgeon's hands than the inert obedience of a forceps or a bistoury. His hands are his most intimate and precious and indispensable assistants— and this in the most literal sense. When he examines a patient, his hands are his surest guides; they alone, by palpation, enable him to establish the direct contact that observation and learning alone could never provide. The things his hand tells him establish this correspondence. In the most realistic sense of the word, the surgeon must know clearly "to his fingertips"; the exactness of his diagnosis and his treatment depend upon his respect for the data his hands bring him. Only his hand can check up on his guesses and presentiments. We cannot doubt its data, for the hand, alone, touches the organs and handles them directly, weighs and feels them. The physician gives close attention to the slightest reactions of his hands; when he deals with an open body, they are more precious to him than the pictures his eyes obtain and the too-abstract ideas his textbooks suggest to him.

Only after his hands have instructed him, initiated him into the elements of a complete diagnosis, or at least that important part of diagnosis called the certitude of control, does the surgeon proceed to action. Here the role of the hands comes into its own. Less spectacular perhaps than that of the musical virtuoso, the "execution" of the surgeon is just as dramatic in its own way. Swift as thought his hand works; it incises, separates, connects, stanches blood, stops losses, redresses, incurves, cuts off, grafts, sutures. A veritable Proteus, it executes all these roles without allowing the least imperfection. If the surgeon's hand cuts, it must handle the bistoury much more surely than the butcher his knife. If the surgeon sews, he must do so with more art than an embroiderer. When he saws or files, it is with a power and delicacy unknown to the most adroit sculptor or cabinetmaker. And all this in record time! The terrible anesthetic imposes a rhythm and a limit that cannot be overreached without grave danger: the surgeon must keep time like a musician. And the marvel is that his hands allow him to do all this. Without this wonderful mastery of his hands, how could he ever venture to operate?

We can define only by the word "venture" this prospecting into the unknown, this constant adaptation to the unforeseen. Sickness is general, but the sick person is unique. There is no place here for assured a prioris, for cocksure arrogance. From force of habit and routine, which could recall similar cases to his mind, the surgeon's hand preserves him. Rather, his hand recalls to his mind and makes him feel with his fingers the uniqueness, the singularity of each individual case; and thus it both safeguards and stimulates his vigilance and his freshness of mind.

If the physician is also a teacher, one of the important points he makes in his teaching concerns the respect that a physician must have for the data obtained by his hands. He insists upon putting his students on guard against hasty conclusions and abstractions. They must learn how to recognize and compensate for, by observations and direct palpations, the inevitable margin of uncertainty which always divides fact from theory. Surgery and art of both the mind and the hand must make them work together.

No physician worthy of the name would attach more than a relative importance to titles honoring pure scholarship; he is a professional man; what does it mean to him whether people take him for a scholar? Reality urges him on and demands his service. And what a reality!—the most painful and bloody there is. He does not wish for any titles that do not give his hands their due. It is with them that lives are saved and bodies mended. Of course knowledge and genius can inspire and direct the hands, but they remain hands—that is, humble living tools, purely physical, but whose work is the finest in the world.

There are infirmities that the most gifted and skillful surgery has not been able to cure even to this day—those that deprive people of the use of one or more senses. The blind, the deaf, the deaf-mutes, the blind deaf-mutes would be forever prisoners of their misfortune if we had not found out how to lead them out of their prison by the hand.

This is the most poignant chapter of the history of the human hand. Here, where science has not yet succeeded, the genius of the heart has discovered and used the resources of direct contact. Since the invention of a kind of language founded on gestures and a kind of writing founded on embossment, we can literally say that, thanks to the hand, "the blind see and the deaf hear." The deaf hear through signs sketched by the hand and seen by the eyes; the blind see by following with a fingertip the various combinations of the Braille alphabet. Since then, despite their disability, the blind and the deaf have, in the concrete sense of the words, the world of learning and even the world of art within reach of their hands.

More moving still is the liberation of the blind deaf-mutes. Without manual contact, their body would be a veritable tomb for their souls. There would be no possibility of expression except the purely animal reactions of instinct—tears or cries. How could we reach and awaken these solitary ones, if not by means of the sense of touch, which can be so subtle and so expressive in the hand? If once, only once, the intelligence of these unfortunate people can grasp the sense of these mute signs, we see how quickly it will utilize the pressures of the hands as a language enriching it day by day. These people come to achieve unbelievable progress, solely by means of the hand. Through the hand they unite themselves to the world by ever more intelligent contacts as they gain greater confidence.

There are examples, undeniable and moving, of the profoundly realistic sense certain expressions take on for the blind deaf-mutes, while for most of us they are only metaphors: "to lead someone by the hand," "to shape the mind," "to caress with our hands a sorrow or a heart," "to confide to the hands a secret," "to put yourself into the hands of another." If they did not live by the letter of such expressions, blind deaf-mutes would have nothing human about them.

Is there anything we do not owe to our hands? Everything comes through them: life and talent, science and art, goodness and mercy, pardon and grace. Faithful and discreet, skillful and durable, from the beginning to the end of our lives they assure the realization of our most secret thoughts and our most personal determinations.

In fact the hand enables men to translate and incarnate their inner resources into works made of a firmer stuff than their own emotions, more enduring than their existence. And that is why we find the hand at the very heart of history. By the works it has realized, the hand makes historic continuity possible. Without it, nothing would remain of the works of yesteryear.

Through the results of manual labor—and only through them—the past not only lives but functions. To each rising generation the past presents itself, a great heritage—oppressive, perhaps, but also undeniable. For better or for worse, with joy or irritation, each one finds the labor of his fathers all done. Even before youth can appreciate its value, this gift of the hand is offered to him as a definite and tested benefaction and as a point of departure: the roads marked, houses built, fields worked, books written, inventions made.

Each one is free to find fault with this heritage, as immense as it is multiform—and with reason; for the good is mingled with the bad and the best with the worst. The world as we find it is made in the image of those who have built it: human as each one is. That is why, though we can criticize what our fathers have done, no one has the right to condemn it or reject it wholly. The hands that built the past were sometimes reprehensible and even criminal. But each one of us is indebted to even the most unworthy of his forebears. Had he left nothing but a record of his faults and errors, each man's hand would have made a positive contribution by pointing out to succeeding generations the experiences to avoid. If history has a sense, it is to the hand that it owes it; without the accomplishments of the hand, humanity would be going around in circles. In good as in evil, the positive works of the past not only spare each generation from having to improvise, but they also mark the advance of the total human effort.

❖

CHAPTER III

Taste

ALTHOUGH people are very much interested in taste, they never agree about it. The bon vivants exalt it; serious minds are suspicious of it. Since this is such a controversial question, the wisest thing is not to try to reconcile contrary opinions. It is better to put taste back into its organic context, to refer it to reality, to understand its exact part and place in the general economy of our physiology.

This method permits us not only to isolate the noncontroversial elements of the notion of taste, but even to understand certain applications of taste in other fields. In fact such applications are intelligible only as extensions of its original sense. Besides, the study of taste, which would seem at first to promise only minor interest, is useful from the cultural point of view, belonging, as it does, to the category of things which most people use frequently but with little discernment.

1.

The sense of taste does not, like touch, extend over the whole body. Its structure is obvious, however, since it consists of a net of papillae spread over the upper side and the tip of the tongue. The situation of these papillae explains their function, which is to perceive the savors of foods.

Taste grasps the forms, the nuances, and the many combinations of these savors: bitterness, sweetness, saltiness, and acidity. But what are these? They are actual properties of foodstuffs, distinct from their nutritive value and caloric content. That much is sure. But we must admit that once we have named the kinds of tastes, we do not know much else. There is no lack of opinions, however: many people have commented on their impressions. But, unlike visual or auditory sensations, those of taste imply the destruction of the object that causes them. Incapable of being verified except by good faith, the appreciations of taste are without appeal against arbitrary decisions. Thus they are ideal material for those gratuitous and fruitless discussions that admit all arguments except those drawn from reality.

The study of the interpretations of flavors can end only in an impasse, but not the study of the two fundamental reactions awakened by the perceptions of taste. With very rare exceptions, and independent of our voluntary dispositions, the contact of food provokes a reflex of pleasure or repulsion. Even before it has been clearly perceived by consciousness, these two movements are felt by the organism and give rise to salivary, muscular, and nervous behaviors that are sharply differentiated.

Now these reactions of pleasure or repulsion are the two means by which taste exercises its influence on the functioning of the body.

Their first effect is to bring out a consciousness of the body's neutrality with regard to the quality of foods. Warned by experience, we know that there are agreeable foods and others which are disagreeable. Nevertheless, in the presence of any nourishment we are only simple, hungry people wanting something substantial and solid. With our appetite is mingled, more or less consciously, an interest in knowing if "this food will be good or bad." Certainly the expectation of pleasure increases our eagerness, but the apprehension of something disagreeable restrains it. We become particular.

Hence the inconveniences and demands which are deplored by intellectuals but which are really the price of a privilege. By the reactions it excites, taste constrains us to a certain discernment. In so doing it protects us from the tyranny of the organic appetite alone, which is greedy and blind. We owe to taste the fact that we do not act like voracious animals in the presence of food. Attention to flavors, in spite of its elementary object, is a taking thought and an application of our powers of choice. By extending the field of our attention to this humble domain—which also belongs to us—the sense of taste contributes in rendering us further present to ourselves; that is to say, it reinforces our organic unit with a psychological unit.

The preferences and dislikes of taste do not proceed exclusively from the whims of gourmandism. They express needs that are deep and silent. They speak in their own way of the demands or repulsions of secret zones of the organism. Far from disdaining them and treating them as fancies, physiology interprets them, knowing that they are motivated by physical needs. We need only to see the differences in assimilative behavior, depending on whether it is a question of a food that pleases or one that displeases.

The will has no power over the actions of glands and muscles. To pretend to ignore completely the warnings of the appetite is an arbitrary act which is not virtuous but dangerous. The real physical needs, the exact organic necessities, are precise conditions of health which cannot be regulated by set rules. The great St. Augustine shows himself wiser than certain moralists when he reminds religious superiors in regard to sick people, "Whatever pleases them, believe me, does them good." (*"Prodesse creditur quod delectat."*)

Passing from the instinctive viewpoint of simple physiological reflexes to the psychological reactions of real life, we discover why satisfactions in eating and drinking have good reason to influence us. Maintaining the body is, for most people, the most wearying and tormenting of all their cares and duties, so much work and weariness, humiliations and pains does it imply. Eating and drinking, which so many fine minds speak highly of, are for the great majority the most relentless servitude of our human condition. If taste, with its simple delights, did not make them see the problem in a less somber light, nourishing the body would be nothing but a bore to us. Thanks to taste, this act of servitude becomes a consolation. A poor good and a very elementary recompense, doubtless—but who, knowing what it would otherwise cost, would dare to belittle it?

Because of the joy they find there, men, primitive or civilized, have in all times made a repast the center and symbol of family intimacy: the gesture of pride where the father sees the result of his labors, since he eats a bread he has earned; the mother's gesture of love, proof of her untiring devotion, doing the same task daily. Around the table tongues are loosed and hearts opened. The table is the place of friendship, of meetings and exchanges, of pleasantries and discussions. To the eyes of the heart, a good meal is a total act, to which a man brings his whole self.

No one can doubt that God wanted it this way. His only Son inaugurated His public life during a meal—a wedding feast—and accomplished His first miracle by changing water into wine, wine that the Psalm affirms "was created to gladden the heart of man." It was in the course of a meal —the last—that He gave to His own His supreme confidences. Under the form of a meal, He pictured to them the joy of meeting in His kingdom: "I shall drink no more the fruit of the vine with you, until we drink it together in the kingdom of God." These, of course, are metaphors, but how eloquent they are, and how foreign to the fears of the water-drinking moralists of both the Old and the New World! This lesson is so dear to the heart of Christ that most of His appearances after the Resurrection took place in the course of a meal. Until the frightful event which tore away the veil that had, until then, hidden His transcendence, the Word made flesh showed Himself always our brother, through the action that is the most simple and indisputable sign of all human solidarity—the partaking of a meal with His own.

2.

At the opposite extreme from the wholly physiological sensations of taste we find that expressions concerning it are used to indicate certain qualities of mind. Exactly what do we mean when we say that someone has good taste or bad taste? This verbal comparison makes us think that, one way or another, it is a question of discernment. In his own field, the man of taste acts like an authentic wine-taster— like a virtuoso in appreciation. This general idea pervades the use of words concerning taste in the cultural order. But we must detail the elements of it.

The expressions "good taste" and "bad taste" indicate dispositions of the mind just as much as the judgments of the mind reveal them. But what judgments are in question? Certainly not those resulting from scientific activity properly so called, for this has its own vocabulary, its own manner of expressing the success or the failure, the worth or deficiency of those who are devoted to knowledge, pure or applied. Scholars are said to have a true mind or a false, a mind that is penetrating or superficial, daring or conservative, precise or wavering—all qualities of strictly intellectual bearing. Knowledge, in fact, has for its exclusive end the penetration and explanation of the very truth of things, of their physical, biological, or metaphysical structure. In the understanding and analysis of beings, lucidity and objectivity of observation, and vigor and rigor of reasoning are the special criteria. Taste, as such, has nothing to say about all this.

Its own appraisals concern aesthetic values. In this field, taste is the correct equivalent of the palate, which discerns the agreeable or disagreeable character of flavors. So taste lets us perceive the beauty or ugliness of beings, the success or failure of their presentation. The judgments of worth which it formulates bear on certain qualities, not on the substance of realities.

The intellectual grasp of the different formulas of beauty goes far beyond the field on which taste as such is exercised. Taste is actually a critical view; it is not content to record; it appreciates, judges, pronounces on the harmony or disharmony of whatever it examines. But, whatever are the standards, there are realities before which it cannot operate in any other way. Reality as such, the world of beings animate or inanimate, escapes human judgment. Its value transcends our preferences, our ideas, and our categories. It expects neither praise nor blame. As disconcerting as it seems to us in its changes, its immense variety is offered for our understanding, but not for our choice. Far from depending on us, it conditions us. We have to open ourselves to its dimensions and grow and enrich ourselves by its possibilities.

This is the normal order which presides over all progress. In the best endowed artist, as in the simplest mind, the sense of beauty must first be nourished and educated, formed and developed. Before deciding and creating, this sense must be awakened and made receptive. Where can it draw from, on what can it lean, if not on real beauty, as it is presented to it by the infinite multitude of existing beings? So taste, unless it wishes to turn into presumptuous, arbitrary complacency, must first be inspired by a humbly attentive receptivity to what it can learn about the objective conditions of true beauty.

Enlightened by this wise circumspection, taste allows itself to judge only works proceeding from human art. Even then, it judges with a sharp sense of the relativity of the things upon which its preference is founded. Taste prefers a conditional presentation of its impressions to a categorical decision. And it does so with so much more good grace if one is himself striving to produce. Impetuous as they may be in showing their preferences, the greatest artists—unlike professional critics, who content themselves with judging the works of others—almost always refrain from unconditional decisions.

Because of the nuances that it never fails to make, good taste is a kind of superior sensitivity of the mind and the heart; it provides them, as it were, with extra antennae by which they can detect the specific data of concrete beauty. Essentially alive, it does not confine itself to any precise canon. Whether it is a question of a house or a piece of furniture, a concerto, a gown, or a perfume, it accommodates itself. It is supple and delicate; it is as whimsical as it is exacting.

In this mixture of nuance and rigor, in fact, lies one of the most astonishing paradoxes of taste: just as in the physiological order it does not decide on flavors by the quality or strength of foods, in the same way in aesthetics it does not judge according to the sumptuosity, opulence, volume, surface, or price of the elements of a work. With merciless lucidity, it sets aside false semblances, discerns equilibrium and imbalance. Like an experienced wine-taster, it knows the secrets of proportions, the mysterious laws of harmony. With an almost infallible sureness it perceives the minute and capricious line of the delicate border beyond which enough becomes too much, and little not enough.

What are the laws inspiring it? Taste knows nothing of laws. It knows too well its own intuitive character to try to justify itself. Its own fastidiousness gives it such a sense of the delicacy of the imponderables to which all success is due, that it is prevented from burdening them with a set of rigid rules.

Current expressions also use the ideas of taste in considering human actions. To act and behave with good taste are requirements which, although they do not raise the standards of morality, arise from a deep understanding of our activity. The aesthete has a word to say about this last, and this he has a good right to do, for human acts are, in their way, a work of art: they are the outward projection of creative talent and of spiritual and moral qualities. Their goodness even belongs to a harmonious orderliness which results, inwardly, in accord with their object, and outwardly in their being correctly placed with regard to circumstances, persons, and surroundings. This total goodness is seen by the moralist from the point of view of the virtues involved; but nothing keeps the aesthete from judging it in the name of the art of living, as a work of beauty and a noble success.

Good taste, in words, actions, or gestures, inspires and brings into being the art that gives us the best things in human relations. But of what does good taste actually consist? Although to the eyes of the moralist it is a synthesis of the good of all the virtues, it is harder to explain than its contrary, bad taste, the cause of so many annoyances and inconveniences, both social and personal. We can sum up the principal characteristics of these irritations.

When it concerns the expression of thought, bad taste is recognized by a lack of proportion between form and depth, content and presentation; then it is called bombast or pomposity. When bad taste destroys the delicacy of manners, it is cynicism or grossness. If it conflicts with subtlety and grace, it is called excess or vulgarity. Its least serious form, often excused by awkwardness or ignorance, is a lack of propriety.

When the aesthete seeks to be precise about the causes of bad taste, he joins forces with the moralist. The faults of bad taste, in art as in conduct, are almost always due only to excess. They reveal pretension and lack of restraint, arrogance, and the egotism of a vain self-love. To make its way at any price, to wish to impose itself on the attention of others and to arouse, if not always admiration, at least the astonishment of others, are the direct consequences of an ego obsessed by itself and the talents it believes itself to have. Nothing, therefore, can save it from exaggeration.

The most amoral aesthete must admit that the virtues at least preserve people from bad taste. Modesty, self-forget-fulness, and the sense of the relativity of his own merits inspire their possessor with that minimum of reserve that avoids ridiculous showing off. Certainly these virtues can-not compensate for lack of talent or genius; but in the absence of these gifts, they do destroy any illusion of pos-sessing them and the temptation to pretend to have them. Moreover, misunderstood as they are, these virtues have, from the simple standpoint of the art of living, the immense merit of engendering, as they do, a horror of presumptuous conceit and immoderacy, and of creating a desire and a concern, in great matters and small, for this supreme condition of all refinement which we call discretion.

From whatever angle we envisage it, and in whatever realm we find it, good taste, mysterious though it may be in its immediate causes, always bears the mark of two distinct sources: a generous heart and a well-disposed soul.

Third Part

❖

THE BODY IN ACTION

❖

❖

❖

❖

CHAPTER I

Movement

1.

WHAT is more commonplace and less interesting than the fact of going and coming, acting and moving, walking and running? We give only the vaguest attention to actions of this kind. They are merely physical effort to us, not matter for reflection.

And the complex of organic dispositions from which they proceed is not generally a part of the principles of human action of interest to moral philosophers. Movements depend on laws that concern physiology and mechanics and elude the conscious will. But this power is a remarkable one, and its activity has numerous profound effects on our psychology. Instinctive and unconscious though it is, our automatic nervous system is never entirely cut off from the man.

Science as such has nothing to do with these interactions. Science is concerned only with the precise field it chooses to analyze. The human observer who wants to understand the uniqueness and the end of this power or that power cannot pigeonhole his researches in this way.

To be capable of moving by oneself is a privilege of the higher living beings. It implies an organic structure that is more complex and more highly developed than the structure (admirable in itself) which assures the maintenance of life. Bodies gifted with the power to move are veritable walking factories, which not only can move about without injury, but have everything to gain by not staying in one place. Such a mechanism is far superior to the most highly perfected apparatus. It appears fragile and is small in size, but is so arranged that it obeys our most unguessable desires. And it does this so readily that we take no account whatever of the maneuvers our wishes impose on the complicated network of bones, articulations, joints, muscles, tendons, and nerves of which the motor apparatus is composed.

This ease and versatility of movement increase with the complexity of living things. The human body is a wonderful masterpiece in this respect. Its skeleton can hold itself erect, keep its balance, lean over and turn, not only easily but with grace. Not a detail does not come together to augment this mingling of strength and elegance. We admire even the structure of the foot. On this supple arch the weight of the body rests, distributed on a triple point of support: the heel, the great toe, and the other toes.

Independence in simple physical movements is the first and the essential sign of the autonomy of the living being, especially the human being. We can literally say that the child begins to count for something and to be considered as an individual from the instant he is able to move about. Mothers know this; so the first steps of their little ones awaken as much alarm as pride.

The child who walks alone detaches himself from his parents; he ceases to be one who depends on direct contact for everything. He disposes his steps; he is himself, irredeemably. Limited as may be the ties he can contract with his fellow beings, an imperceptible distance separates him from them. Restricted as he may be, he still remains one who can go away. On his own part, he must keep account of the autonomy of moving around and of the actions of those he believes would forestall him or hold him back. Independence of motion is truly the symbol of the relativity of the power we can exercise over one another.

Locomotion, while it assures our independence, is not an entirely free activity. Rather than being matter for caprice and whim, the exercise of our possibilities, even our physical possibilities, is governed by necessity. It is our destiny as men to be able to move about where and when it seems good to us, but also to be constrained according to our needs. We are obliged to meet halfway the beings and things we need. And this in every way and for this reason: "Who wishes to survive must start moving."

So, like the verbs "to be" and "to have," the verb "to go" is one of the most fundamental in all human languages.[1] What action is not more or less explicitly so called? Except for the interior action of the mind and heart, our acts imply a movement—that is, a moving

---

[1] Their use is so constant that, in every language, these three verbs (to the despair of students) are irregular. The variety of forms does away with the impression of repetition and monotony.

around, partial or total. To survive and to advance in life imply that a human being will put himself out; to move is a fundamentally necessary function.

This elementary compulsion has sent man everywhere. Interest, curiosity, hunger, and thirst (and many other reasons also) have made him an incessant traveler. Where has he not visited, inventoried, prospected? Where has he not settled? Here we touch on one of the most impressive aspects of the adventure of the human race. Although it is more delicate, fragile, and defenseless than most animal (and vegetable) constitutions, man's body reveals an absolutely unique resistance and tenacity. It is shown, by evidence, to be capable not only of surviving, but also of resisting and adapting itself to the worst conditions. In places where beasts and plants cannot exist, the human body lives and works! In the most literal sense of the words, man is the only being that is geographically universal; while other species perish beyond certain latitudes and longitudes, he acclimates himself everywhere.

Roads are good witnesses of this courage and this endurance. An innumerable network of them encompasses the world, almost as old as the earth and always kept in repair, for there is an enduring law urging us to make our lives an uninterrupted march in space and time.

2.

In so using its own strength, the human body finds its proper vital equilibrium. Immobility and stagnation are fatal to it. If, for one reason or another, the body does not move about and exercise, an unhealthy lassitude soon appears. The body becomes heavy and dull, the blood thickens, and the machinery creaks. We are so made that everything in us should work together, if not in equality, at least closely enough to avoid any discrepancy among our various activities.

It is useless to pretend to escape from this unity of the human complex, even under the pretext of intensifying intellectual or spiritual activity. To neglect physical exercise (and all that this implies of plunging into concrete reality and the positive conditions of life) has curious consequences sometimes: notably, that of mistaking the ideas secreted in a vacuum for Absolutes in the name of which we decide and judge all things. Gratuitous abstraction and intellectual pretension are often the price we pay for lack of a physical airing out. Realism, enrichment, and renewing of our mental landscapes depend to a certain extent on our contacts with new people and new things.[2]

Stagnation frequently leads to narrow-mindedness (which appreciates nothing but what it is used to: *my* town, *my* environment, *my* traditions); in opposition to this, travel obliges us to take account of the fact that other things exist and that these other things have value. They permit the mind to open, to record, to acquire a sense of distinctions and of differences; that is to say, intellectual probity and justice. On condition, of course, that they are not in the least like those travels which are inspired only by the snobbish desire to accumulate mileage in record time. The most fruitful travels have never been the longest or the swiftest. Changes of horizon are of intellectual profit only to those whose curiosity remains attentive and receptive and, above

[2] It would be interesting to examine and compare systems, philosophical or otherwise, as affected by the kind of life their authors lead.

all, those whose spiritual honesty is large enough to drive back the instinctive prejudices that are always ready to interpret arbitrarily—while misjudging—whatever surprises or disconcerts them. All this demands time, both to record and to try to understand, although when we have formed the habit we can see better. Then a rhythm of change can be in tune with our sensory and mental faculties. But, as all real observers avow, those who have known how to discover the richness of the world—going on foot is the most perfect way of learning.

To convince ourselves of this, we have only to compare the sense of observation and the respect for the objective data of reality possessed by peasants or mountain dwellers (who must always go on foot) and that of motorists from proud cities. The comparison does not flatter the city-dweller. Many, more and more, feel the need of refreshing spiritual and physical health by tramping the roads.

The art of walking and the art of strolling—veritable scandals to the eyes of hurried, serious men—have always been the delight of great workers. Besides being a relaxation which allows the mind to regain calm, they offer leisure for gathering impressions that a more rapid and efficient progress does not permit us to record. How many details and nuances we discover as soon as we begin to take our time!

It is not only knowledge that we gain from walking. Noble sentiments are united with a fondness for the mountains and the sea. The taste for high summits does not go with a soft or superficial nature. The joys of alpinism are the result of rude effort; hence their purifying and health-giving value.

Without this ability to move, what would happen to our meetings with other people? We cannot meet others unless we move about. To meet one another, men must go to one another. Thought or desire is not enough. All relationship implies at least a minimum of going out. To visit a friend is the very first manifestation of the interest we have in him. To go with him is not an empty gesture; it shows an attentive solicitude.

What is more eloquent, in their simplicity, than the many expressions where our spiritual and moral attitudes are united to the idea of going? "For his sake I would go to the ends of the world," "He followed a bad road," "We shall go on to the end," or the vulgar but significant, "I made him get a move on."

The Gospel brings us a witness of the incarnation of our own feelings in showing us Our Lord as *viator*. Christ has good reason for wishing His most spiritual biographer, St. John, to mention the fatigue of His travels along the roads of Palestine and Galilee. On the day after His Resurrection, we see Him walking along the way to Emmaus with His disciples. He wished to know and partake of all the pains of men. Following them and in their company, He traveled roads and paths. In the most physical, painful, and harassing sense of the words, He associated Himself in all their comings and goings. Even as a little child, He knew the actual road of exile. Heavily weighted, He climbed the road to Calvary.

Since these things came to pass, a Christian no longer sees the roads of the world in the same light. They are still the way and the symbol of travel and of exile, of wars and of wanderings, of daring and of adventure. But since God made flesh has followed them, they are blessed. Upon them shines another light than that of the sun, other steps are printed there than those of cupidity and hatred, ambition and cruelty—the steps of the messengers of justice and charity. Above all, they have lost their despairing aimlessness. Long and entangled though they may be, they are no longer purely terrestrial. They lead somewhere! Since hope has been revealed, the march through time has ceased to be a wandering. It has a meaning, which is to lead us to God and to prepare us for His encounters. And Faith teaches us that, the full length of the road, a Witness walks with us, One who knows every winding and every difficulty. When we join Him, He shall judge us, not as a spectator or a master of courses, but as a companion in travel and in misery.

CHAPTER II

Play and Sport: Free Movement

THE necessities of life and the requirements of our physical and mental health make us exert ourselves. Sometimes, in spite of the energy we use in works of this sort, there is still a surplus of energy (at least during our youth) which we can dispose of in any way we like best. We judge the vigor and the health of a body by its command of a capital of strength in excess of the requirements of the instinct for self-preservation and necessary labor.

The ways in which people make use of this overflow of vitality do not always seem reasonable to temperaments that are calmer or, often, less rich in energy. Minds that are too rational are disconcerted by the turbulence of a vigorous child and by the sportive prowess of adults.

They think that efforts leading only to mock victories are useless and exaggerated. They talk about the exaltation of the body to the detriment of the mind. They find that the motives involved are too superficial and the ideal of sport is unworthy of mankind. Are they right? Are the play of the child and the sport of the adult really nothing but a pure and simple exaltation of animality? Whoever takes the trouble to examine them more closely is not so sure. The meaning of these things may be hidden, but it seems to be more real and often deeper than their detractors say.

1.

The bodily movements to which a child devotes himself are really quite reasonable. In season and out of season, he comes and goes, runs and jumps, throws himself about as if moved by forces he does not yet know how to control. His turbulence is directly proportionate to his vitality.

As unreflecting as it may be, this exuberance is never wholly animal. To anyone who asks him why his prowess or his foolishness, he always answers, "I am having fun; I am playing this or that." Along with his legs and his arms his imagination is working, giving a meaning to his movements and justifying in his own eyes his most ridiculous impulses. He builds for himself a world of his own where he plays a part that is, without his knowing it (happily), the projection of his vitality. His answers are often called stupid excuses by those who ask him to give an account of them—especially those resulting in some damage to property. Educators should understand that these explanations are the first workings of a still-unskilled mind dealing with an activity directly inspired by instinct. To the observer (if not to the parents!) they are naïve and moving evidence of the presence, in this little rascal, of something transcendent which the banal will never satisfy. The child cannot move without feeling a need to justify and adorn all that he does. Already he cannot bear the absurdity of the useless.

People who advocate absurdity—philosophers or romancers—would gain much by watching and listening to small children playing.

2.

Human beings, when they are adult, cannot fall back on such childish justifications for their need of using up their surplus of vital energy. The mind has awakened to ideas which, if not better founded, are at least more serious; so they usually have a sort of false shame that prevents them from admitting that the efforts expended in their games are really useless.

Aside from this, desires and passions are born which find in physical exertions a chance to exercise themselves: passions of contesting and risking, dominating and being victorious. So organized, play becomes sport. But, at bottom, the activity here, as there, remains the same: a consumption of energy from which the whole idea of productivity and material gain is excluded. In this it differs from the useful activity of working. It is inspired rather by a wish to obtain some special result from the strength of the body.

People who are opposed to sports welcome the opportunity to denounce all that kind of thing as a glorification of the body. They forget that in the course of history sports activities have often been stressed to compensate for some organization of life which does not recognize just physical needs. In times when mechanical inventions have more and more reduced the physical labors of work, exercises of sport have become the only means of compensating for the absence of the physical exertions the body requires.

The sportive spirit is evidently not marked by the great and stirring ideals of pure thought. But the althlete does not pretend to this. It is a remarkable thing, in fact, that the most enthusiastic supporters of athletics have never tried to make it the supreme end of life. They do not try to conceal the fact that success in this field can be obtained only during a certain period of life—the time of greatest physical vigor—and that these successes are only temporary. The feeling of their being only temporary rules so strongly that the vanity born of victories has not time to turn into true pride. How many ideals—artistic, philosophical, political, or even religious—furnish to their faithful followers so effective an antidote against the pretentious conceit of success?

Underlying all athletic contests we find, more or less admitted, a desire for victory. Upon this is grafted the hope of outstanding achievement that awakens human vainglory. But, unlike what too often happens elsewhere, the satisfaction of self-love is not easy in these fields; it demands brute efforts. Pretension and verbal boasting become ridiculous. All that counts is the positive results which can be recorded, indisputable proof which can be given by the athlete himself. Of all the many forms of human competitions, sport remains one of the rare ones in which official success goes to the real victor.

The vanity of those who win has at least the excuse of resting on merits which are true and which are their own. Athletic contests have laws whose strict observance conditions the lawfulness and confirmation of victories. Most of them have remained aloof from the little trickeries that sully certain sports. The sense of fair play is so strong that even those who engage in sordid dealings must take care to respect appearances; so they render homage to the fundamental honesty of sport.[1]

Before we talk about the feelings of the contestants, let us try to find out just why they have chosen the principal sports to which they devote themselves. This is what we may call the question of the objective conditions of sport.

To prove their strength, men choose ways to test it. Here the instinct for battle inspires them. Whatever seems to hinder them or to be an obstacle awakens and stimulates reactions of combativity, at least where there is vigor and vitality. So we see men taking pride in play, forcing themselves to the easy accomplishment of movements and actions that are painful and difficult, and even to brave certain causes of their troubles. *Distance* and *time*, which bridle and restrain our desire for haste, become two enemies which they defy and whose control they seek to reduce.

Dreams of swiftness have always haunted the imaginations of men. To go where it seems good to them, as rapidly as possible, appears as a triumph over their condition as walking animals obliged by their structure to advance only step by step. Their phobia against slowness is so great that it has been one of the most efficient stimuli of inventiveness. To diminish fatigue and to accelerate quickness, the mind has multiplied its discoveries.

But rather than mechanical triumphs the true sportsman

[1] "Hypocrisy is the tribute vice pays to virtue."

prefers the modest victories that his own body accomplishes and benefits by. A foot runner can make better time only if his whole body is improved: his gait must be broken in, his pace must become more regular, and he must be able to breathe more deeply and have better breath control. He is conscious of his progress and enjoys it to a degree unknown to jet pilots who can travel faster than sound. The foot track awakens a true and healthy fervor; it has its solitary adepts, even some famous champions who have established their records without needing the stimulus of official competitions.

To conquer his own weight, to know, more than he possibly can, the tirelessness and lightness of a bird, is one of the other great dreams of man. The mind permits him to compare his condition with that of others, and so rouses ambitions which, whether visional or wise, show how much we suffer from the limitations imposed on us.

In literature, the need to escape from the servitude of weight gave rise to the myth of Icarus, whose fall always seems, not a just punishment for his temerity, but a horrible and shabby revenge taken by jealous gods. Several decades ago this ancient dream finally came true. For once, at least in its beginnings, a human invention was born of the union of human genius and the spirit of adventure and risk, of the desire—which serious people thought childish, but which is really so right and innocent—to fly, to play at being a bird. For reasons that are, alas, much less pure, this great invention has progressed so far that man has become, if not the complete master of space, speed, and height, at least one who can use them without constraint.

In contrast to the enormous distances of aviation, but

born of the same desire to conquer mass and weight, we
find the art of the high jump. Compared to those of certain animals, the results attained by man seem ridiculous.
Let us think what they involve. The structure of the human
skeleton does not favor vertical effort. The muscular trigger-
ing by which the body tears itself from the ground has only
two centers and two points of balance, instead of the four
at the disposal of animals. So, in proportion, the athlete
who raises his own weight to the height of his body has
accomplished, at least from the anatomical point of view,
a real feat.

More spectacular and more impressive are acrobatics in
their various forms. To muscular power the gymnast, the
acrobat, and the trapezist must unite—and to what a degree!—suppleness and agility, sureness and quick reflexes,
daring cool-headedness, and mastery of wind and nerves.
They play their bodies like a virtuoso. Their feats are so
many wagers against the laws of rigidity and weight. The
cadence and grace they show amid the worst difficulties
and most painful efforts often make us forget the harshness
of the training required. The ordinary spectator grasps
nothing but the beauty and picturesqueness of circus acts.
The most amazing thing escapes his notice: the living symphony of muscles which, by strength of courage and daring,
a human being can achieve with his body.

Besides these highly skilled exercises there are others,
minor manifestations of athletics, such as javelin-throwing,
discus-throwing, weight-lifting. Here muscular power must
be allied to the art of managing and directing one's
strength.

The lifters of weights and of dumbbells are the poor relations of the sport world. Their efforts bear directly on the large muscles, and increase not only the power but the size of these muscles, so that they are often ungraceful. They know it. They do not dare to appear in the stadium, where comparison with athletes (whose development of the long muscles favors slimness) would make them look ridiculous. They are content to show at fairs and carnivals. The spectators there are less exacting, and above all they are more capable of appreciating the power of movements which they can see are something like their own. These modest "strong men," brothers of those who work by main strength, are a little like poets in their way—poets of the hardest work there is.

For many reasons men have also braved the water. They have made a real epic poem of this duel with an element so different from their own, where the victories are many and striking enough to compensate for and even to make us partly forget the too-frequent tragedies. Technical skill has made the rivers and seas truly extensions of the highways on the land.

The sport of swimming is only a humble and individual transposition of the complex and imposing art of navigation. Beautiful triumph of the solid over the fluid! The craft and discipline of movements reverse the order of things; movements in the water have a variety, an efficacy, and a grace which walking on firm ground can never possess. The body has made an ally of fluidity, which normally would be fatal to it.

❖

Mental skill has enabled human physical bodies to triumph over difficulties and rule over things they could not dominate directly, such as the water and the air.

In a similar way, man has also confronted animals. For man has made himself a trainer of beasts, for pleasure as well as from necessity. Although he is less robust and less swift than most of them, he has known how to use their superior physique to his profit. And in order to prove his ascendancy over them, he has gone so far as to make the most ferocious animals perform tricks at his command.

The art of taming wild beasts is a true department of sport. But this time the movements are done by others. The spectacles of the circus, a feast for the eyes and a source of quite unique emotions, are an amazing demonstration of the primacy of human intelligence, which is capable of directing not only man's own body, but even the bodies of wild beasts.

Let us think of the conditions and the lesson of this taming. It implies an authority which excludes the use of force, which would terrorize, or violence, which would harm. Confidence is basic to its success. The beasts obey only those whom they feel are their friends. Here, above all, patience and gentleness assure success. Saint-Exupéry was not wrong in the way he approached the miracle of the friendship which leads the heart of man to tame wild beasts:

> "What does it mean, to tame?" asked the little prince.
> "It is a thing too much forgotten," said the fox. "It means, to create ties."
> "Create ties?"
> "Yes, surely," said the fox. "You are nothing to me yet

but a little boy like a hundred thousand other little boys. And I have no need of you. You have no need of me, either. I am only a fox to you, like a hundred thousand other foxes. But if you tame me, we shall need each other. You would be, for me, unique in the world. I should be to you unique in the world."

The fox fell silent and looked a long while at the little prince.

"Please, tame me!" he said.

"I would like to," said the little prince. "But I have not enough time. I have friends to discover and many things to learn."

"One knows only the things which one tames," said the fox. "Men have not time to know anything. They buy things ready-made at the stores. But as there are no merchants who sell friends, men have no friends any more. If you wish to have a friend, tame me!"

"What must I do?" asked the little prince.

"You must be very patient," said the fox.

3.

An indissoluble friendship, in the sporting clubs, links the champion who always comes in first and the champion who always comes in second; the latter by admiration, the former by generosity. No chain is more powerful than this half-meter of space. Pylades was one who leaped a little less high than Orestes, and Patroclus one whom Achilles always beat by a chest.—Jean Giraudoux.

We have analyzed the kinds of sport; now we shall analyze the mentality it implies or awakens in the contestants. Competitions of sport are battles against competitors; emulation and a wish to conquer play a leading part in them.

This explains the fighting and ever-warlike character of the vocabulary used in describing matches and combats. Words about adversaries, victory, defeat, and sometimes ruin, abound in the descriptions given. Always, outrageous as they may be, this verbal tragedy allows the use of dramatic terms. There are accidents, involuntary and always condemned; aside from these, the blows received do not wound, are not meant to cripple, and still less meant to kill. The most infuriated fight and the roughest combat must succeed in the tour de force (which leaves the philosopher dumbfounded) of "annihilating" an adversary without "destroying" him. At the end of a trial of strength where he has succumbed, the most defeated, the most humbled, the most overwhelmed loser can still smile.

People who think they have good taste call this language ridiculous. Why do they not make an effort to find out what actually inspires it? Its very immoderation betrays it. Cold reason ceases to weigh its words, often so insulting and annoying. Hatred is prudent and astute in its bitterness; but the language of sport is innocent of such calculation; its exaggerations are only those of childhood, where violence and outrageous language have nothing scornful or wicked about them. In the heart of all their disputes and squabbles, the most excited street boys would not for anything in the world do one another any real harm.

So battles in sport, which appeal to the combative passions, formally exclude the bad feelings existing in real warfare. Men who wish to imitate and conquer one another do not treat their competitors as enemies. They keep their purity, by the very nature of things. Indeed, as compared with what happens in bloody combat, in which it is necessary to arouse contempt and hatred for the enemy (for we seek to destroy only what is ominous and evil), mutual respect is the very real condition of success in all true sporting competitions. The opponents are all equals; they confront one another only because they belong in the same category. Who would fight with a physical inferior? This would be cowardice. A victory is not praiseworthy unless it is difficult, obtained over an adversary you think is superior to yourself. Hence there is an inherent nobility in all combats of this kind.

Brutality as such has no place in these contests, where our bodies draw upon its entire capital of strength and energy. Violence must be disciplined. For the efficiency of every movement depends, above all, on the tactical skill that inspires and directs it. But the tactic is in the mind, and the mind sees clearly only when it keeps calm. The very nature of the struggle forces the adversaries to refrain from giving way to the anger that excitement might awaken in them.

To the end of a battle so fought, the victor, knowing the qualities of his opponent, keeps his respect for him; for the worth of his opponent establishes his own merit. And defeat itself has nothing on which resentment or spite can properly feed. If the rules have been kept, there is no dishonor in ceding to an adversary who has proved his superiority. To belittle the one who has defeated you would be so evident an absurdity that the blindest pride would perceive it; how can you call a man mediocre when he has defeated you without seeing that you are even more mediocre? The loser can blame no one but himself, and reproach himself with his lack of form or preparation. Willy nilly, a defeat in sport has the rare merit of putting to the test the opinion a man has of himself.

When the sporting competitions are between opposing groups, success implies a concerted effort demanding special qualities from the teammates, qualities that we call team spirit.

To the authentic mentality of sportsmanship, which wants each man to put forth his best efforts, team spirit adds a brief but important limitation: *in his own place*. It is not the right thing any more for each individual to try to lead or play the chief part. A true team member is a modest man, capable of recognizing the ability that allows his companions to take a place where he would be less apt.

He must know how to do his share in full measure, but by integrating in the maneuver of the whole and by forgetting himself to aid his teammates. Without preaching or posing, every good teammate is truly generous. While not always so refined as in the polite world, comradeship arising from team spirit contains a sincerity of rapport which is too real to be treated lightly. In our own day we see that a great many movements intended to promote causes more noble than sport are begging people to take sport as a good model of working together. They imply that games and sports have made people work together better than many of their own ideals have been able to do.

4.

The feelings that are awakened in the public as they watch sporting events are not always noticeably elegant. Those accustomed to literary reunions or society gatherings often think they have a right to disdain the behavior so dear to the crowds, as if the games of the stadium are not to be compared, in health or propriety, with the distractions in which refined people take their pleasure.

The fans of the sport world, seen in full action, certainly do not present a picture of sedateness. Restraint is not a virtue of the out-of-doors. The public of the cycle-race track, the ring, or the stadium thinks of other things than self-control. Literally carried away by the game —at least if it is a good one—the public has no self-control whatever. The slightest variations in the course or the match awaken in all of them emotions they express by shouts, howls, and frantic encouragements or imprecations.

The mere objective interest of the spectacle taking place is not enough to explain such vehemence. Letting loose these collective passions is, above all, a part of the essentially combative nature of sporting competitions. They are peaceful, but they touch warlike fibers. The great merit of sport really lies in the peaceful outlet it offers that instinct and in the imaginary activity accompanying it. Thanks to this, men can experience all the emotions of actual combat, without bloodshed, and with much more violence because they are felt in a group. Everything is amplified by the collective coefficient. The gregarious spirit carries it beyond self-control; once he has entered the door of the stadium, each man is only a partisan; nothing exists for him or for the others but the defense of a certain camp. So men shout themselves hoarse and scream invective, and nobody dreams of being offended by any of it. The fever of sport anesthetizes individual self-love.

Along with the match of the players, occasioned and affected by it, goes another, in which the spectators are the actors. Never, even in the heroic times of face-to-face combat, has the field of battle known such mighty clashes. Gusts of passion go from man to man, from bench to bench, from gallery to gallery, but they thrill chiefly the ears that hear them and the throats that utter them. Everybody experiences all sorts of emotions, and, in the end, feels the intoxication of the common victory or sinks into the depression of tragic catastrophe.

This adventure seems childish when we view it in cold blood. What would the city be, though, if those great and terrible children that are men could not free themselves in this way from their warlike instincts? These relatively peaceful manifestations let them experience (on a local, national, or even an international scale) moments of extreme excitation for which ordinary life gives little occasion, but which must take place to purge the feelings men have in spite of themselves. The old Greeks, who knew men, said that the spectacles of the stadia purged the animal passions and humors. Really they furnish an occasion, positive and inoffensive, to exercise them. Irascibility, which underlies and irritates so many feelings, runs less risk of turning into bile when it is used up in shouting. Promoters of games and matches, and the competitors and the journalists, contribute to the eliminating of the moral poisons of the city. One bit of evidence is that in wartime, when all reserves of anger must be mobilized, spectacles and propaganda of sport take a second place.

To know the temper of a nation, we must observe its favorite spectacles. The stadium and the arena furnish just as sure documentation as any official report.

The nations of the north, less nervous or more self-controlled, enjoy calmer distractions than those demanded by nations of the Mediterranean regions. Those of the south take delight in games the northerners find barbarous. But without bullfights what would serve them for an outlet, what would become of the fierce violence which, without their seeking it, the Spanish and their neighbors have in their blood? The Church knows this, and so she underlined the reasons for her condemnation.

In its interdiction of bullfights, the Church's point of view is entirely different from that of the societies for the protection of animals—whose members too often, let it be said in passing, are more careful of beasts than of their human brothers. The Church does not waste time lavishing an excessive tenderness on animals. Although she knows that the arena is practically a butcher's stall, she does not find any more to complain about than for the bull killed in the slaughterhouse. On the contrary. At least, before his death, the bull of the bullfight has had every chance; nothing impedes him, and he keeps his formidable strength to the end. So her condemnation of the bullfight is entirely for the protection of man. Not because he plays a game that is in itself dangerous—if this were the case the Church would forbid everything involving a useless risk, which she has never done—but because the circumstances are such that the most skillful toreador can be exposed to the danger of losing his self-control and not being able to fight adequately. In order to understand this, one must have been present at a putting to death. A matador, even one with nerves of steel, cannot long resist the environment of the cries of a crowd in delirium, drunk with sun and emotion, enthusiasm and fury. Many toreadors, losing their calmness, surrender to a recklessness that destroys them. Profound psychologist that the Church is, she has undertaken to protect toreadors against those two unleashed brutes—the bull and the crowd.

Other sports are more peaceful, at least in appearance. Neither boxing nor "catch" involves putting to death. Are they any more gracious or noble than bloody bullfights?

All sporting spectacles, even the more violent ones, succeed in the measure in which they avoid bestial brutality. Intelligence should direct strength and dexterity; skill in maneuvering always goes beyond mere muscular power. The least competition in sport requires efforts so much out of the ordinary that only those can face it whose will and courage are able to impose severe discipline on their bodies —minor manifestations of the rulership of mind over body, no doubt, but at least clear and honest.

Severe moralists are sometimes uneasy about the pride that may be produced in those who excel at sports. Have they ever thought that this pride is much less than the con-

ceit and arrogance of intellectual pride? Athletes know so
well how limited and temporary their triumphs are. The
champion of the hundred-yard dash knows that he is not
champion of the four-hundred-yard race; the feather-
weight knows he is not the champion heavyweight. In
quality and in duration, every victorious athlete knows
his limits; the most brilliant records may be surpassed on
the morrow.

Why should we belittle and becloud these humble joys?
They make up a part of the very rare satisfactions of the
world here below which a man can say that he has, in strict
justice, merited. And not at the price of the unhappiness
of others. The ambition they have is not a superior virtue,
but at least it forces them to pay for their honors in their
own persons. It obliges the athlete to impose on himself
the effort, the discipline, and the constancy indispensable
to all serious preparation for the victor's crown. These are
modest virtues, but they are real ones.

The excessive praise accorded to champions are somewhat scandalous when we think how little praise is bestowed upon artistic or moral worth. But these acclama-
tions, coming from simple men, have a justification we
must recognize and explain. The common people are
enemies of fine words; they judge men by their real acts.
Solemn titles impress them less than a work well done; so
spontaneously they choose their heroes not in the world of
politics or finance, literature or authority (even religious),
but among the "boys" of the stadium and the track, whose
good work they can understand and admire.

St. Paul knew very well what the men of his time
thought about these things; so he assigned the life of the

runner in the stadium as a model of spiritual courage. This argument is more direct and more effective than many sermons preached by many successors of the Apostle of Nations.[1]

[1] *Translator's note:* My attention has been called to the address of Pope Pius XII to the Italian National Congress on Problems of Sports. "Sound doctrine teaches us respect for the body," says the Holy Father, "but not an esteem that is more than just. The maxim is this: care of the body, strengthening of the body, yes; cult of the body, divinization of the body, no. The primacy in the human composition does not belong to the body . . . but to the spirit, to the spiritual soul. . . . The principal and determining factor in the harmonious movements of the members in gymnastics, in the agile and well-planned displacement of players in games, in the powerful grips of muscles in wrestling, in not the body but the soul. In sport and gymnastics, therefore, as in the music of the artist, the principal, dominating element is the spirit, the soul—not the instrument, the body. It is, therefore, the duty of all those devoted to sport to preserve this proper conception of sport—not indeed to disturb or lessen the joy they derive therefrom, but to preserve them from the danger of neglecting higher duties connected with their dignity and respect for God and themselves. Return, therefore, to your enjoyment in the proper use of gymnastics, sport, and rhythmical exercises. Bring to the people their benefits, in order that the health of body and of mind may develop always more and more, and that their bodies may be invigorated for the service of the soul."

❖

CHAPTER III

Dancing: Sublimation
of Movement

Sanctuary, sanctuary, O my sanctuary, O whirlwind! I was in thee, O movement, outside of all things.—Valéry.

1.

HUMAN ACTIONS are varied and changing; and their history is one with that of the energy and ingenuity of the race in its struggles with life. Learned men record with some emotion the incessant evolution and ephemeral character (in spite of their originality or charm) of many manifestations that have disappeared with time. But some activities we find always the same, no matter how far we reach in space or time; among these are the fundamental movements of life and the two universal signs of human relationships which we call war and dancing.

The variations these have both gone through are superficial; war is always war, and dancing is always dancing.
They endure because they take their constancy from life—
the life which the first destroys and the second radiates.
They are the inseparable companions of our history, and
they are so closely related to our misfortune and our happiness that we cannot speak of them with indifference.

We shall not mention war here, except as it is a shadowy
and bloody replica of the dance; war expresses the bitterest
part of our destiny, and the dance fulfills one of the hap-
piest needs of our nature. In all latitudes and at all times
dancing is a manifestation of the health and happiness of
living.

Moralists are often too severe about dancing. Its violence and impulsiveness, its excitement and wantonness
have sometimes made it a dangerous stimulant to the most
questionable tendencies. Moralists have been right to denounce its dangers, and their advice is wise. But dancing
so perfectly satisfies our physical desires that usually these
exhortations have been in vain. Condemnations, even
those uttered in the name of a perfectly good ideal, count
for nothing against the call of instinct. Lax consciences
are only moved to ridicule by preachings against the dance.

As with many human activities, the dance can be divided into the best and the worst. Far from being evil in
itself, it is, rather, an exercise whose meaning and value
most people do not know. To show them its good qualities is just as urgent as to rest content with pointing out
its dangers, and probably more useful. If people knew
the true quality of the dances to which they yield them-

selves, perhaps they would know that they must see them as something more than the purely instinctive use of excess vitality; for dancing, in its essence, is one of the noblest manifestations of the imprint of the mind upon the body.

Ordinary dancers know nothing but its superficial aspect. They execute the figures and the steps without even asking the meaning of what they are doing. They know only that they give themselves up to a motion whose variations and essentially agreeable appeal are to them a sort of "play" on the border of ordinary activity and different in every way from the common movements of walking and working.

Although confused, their intuition is right. Dancing is first of all a happy use of the body, a source of recreation and joy. Whatever the effort it requires, dancing is really a holiday for the body. It has no other end than itself; it is "a useless exercise," and this is its originality and its dignity. So men desire it without mental reservations, and without constraint. We dance in order to dance, as we sing or we laugh: for nothing except the pleasure of dancing, singing, or laughing.

But in this gratuity lie both the charm and the value of the dance. This explains why its attraction is so deep. It is a triumph over the constraints of utility, man's proof that he is not an animal entirely absorbed in organic function. It confirms his fullness of life. So we see that dancing springs from the vitality of a being conscious of possessing enough resources in himself to be able to spend some of them for pleasure alone, to show his freedom, to affirm his independence of the efforts to which the necessities of life compel him.

That is why he instinctively wants dancing to be as unlike useful actions as possible. He spontaneously gives it an inspiration and measure, an ordering and rhythm quite different from that of working, a rhythm whose cadence and appeal are born of the purest and freest wellspring that can exist: music.

Who says music says grace, fluidity, pure melody. The dance surely participates in these qualities in its own way —the way of bodily movements—but with such authenticity that no one dreams of confusing the expressions and the attitudes of dancing with those of the actions dictated by necessity. Dancing is to physical effort what poetry is to prose. Materially, in both cases, the components are identical. The attitudes and movements, like the nouns and adjectives, are in both cases the same. But there is a world of difference between them.

Those who understand this are forced, in spite of their prejudices, to admit that in its essence dancing is never vulgar. By its whole nature it is something different. Its motions and expressions, attitudes and steps are ennobled, precisely because they are withdrawn from their habitual end to be submitted to a purer rhythm.

"The dancer seems to count out and value in coins of pure gold what we spend carelessly as small change—the steps we use whenever we walk for any end whatsoever," said Valéry, who, here as in many other fields, has said the words that require no comment.

The origin and inspiration, measure and style of the dance come from something higher than mere carnal vitality. As important and primal as the part of the body may be, dancing is more than a simple, instinctive vibration. It is the living proof, not always fully conscious but undeniable, of the privilege which a human being's power of movement possesses—to be inspired directly by harmony.

We know that some dances exist which are provoked only by the instinctive urge of the passions of the moment. We may be tempted to see nothing in them but the outward projection of excess vitality. But if we take pains to analyze them later we must see that, whatever type they are, youthful or wild, a child's rounds, or Negro dances, their apparent lawlessness is always subject to rhythm. They imply a cadence, a submission to a discipline to which alone a sensibility superior to pure instinct can yield.

It is rhythm, and not caprice, which imposes charm on the steps, form to their movements, and measure on the whole dance. There is a great abyss between the serpent who, under the influence of the snake-charmer's flute, balances himself, always with the same movement, and the dancer who more or less consciously follows the sinuosities and the time of the melody. With the snake, we are in the presence of the shapeless and mechanical reaction of a stimulated organism; with the dancer, we are concerned with the adaptations (if not willful, at least conscious) of a person capable of yielding himself to the various nuances of the music he hears. The movements of the serpent are only spasmodic, but the dancer's movements form a figure having a meaning.

I do not know what evidence can be drawn (writes Jacques Rivière) from all the bizarre and violent forms composed by dancers. Yes, this one is clear and facile; it has taken on the very contours of what should be conveyed. Here the emotion represented before us is designed, fixed. It lies there like the figure of a great doll the dancer leaves behind him as he goes on. Nothing is more moving than this physical image of the passions of the soul. It is quite another thing than their expression in articulate language. Not only because there are greater depths and more notations of detail and shadows of meaning than are contained in words, but because by this perceptible figure we are brought closer to those emotions, we are brought into their presence in a more immediate fashion, we contemplate them before we can express them in language, before they are surrounded by the countless and expressive but chattering crowd of words. No need to translate, it is not a symbol from which we must pass on to the thing itself. But we are present in the night of the intelligence; we are there with our bodies, and it is the body which understands. A certain awareness, a certain inward recognition . . . Each movement of the dancer is like a word that resembles me. If it sometimes seems strange to me, it is so only to the eyes of my mind, for from the first it enters into my own limbs and into the depths of my body, in a low harmony that is full and perfect.

2.

There is a deeper reason for the variety of dances than diversity of movements alone. Its many outward variations originate in the nuances of inspiration that emotions obey. We cannot dream here of giving a systematic outline of the names of dances, which are legion. Let it be enough for us—for this was our first plan—to discern the stages and even the degrees of quality from which the different dances arise.

On a low plane we find spontaneous and primitive dances, which are born of the need of showing the simple joy of living and of releasing, in their suppleness and variety, energies which more or less bubble out of the body. Although instinct seems to rule this outburst of movement, its animal nature is enlightened by rhythm.[1]

In another order, also instinctive, we find collective dances which, especially in olden times, were inspired by battle and great moments in the life of peoples. Such are war dances and victory dances, which expressed the common courage or joy, creating an environment in which hearts were fused and energies exalted.

Less tragic and less pathetic are the dances we call "narquoises," where men take up again, but under a freer and more lively mode, the very motions of work and weariness. Such are the popular dances, the folk dances, most of which are the joyful conclusion of great labors after harvest or vintage. They are the retaliation of the body refusing to admit fatigue, an evasion of the harassments of the day's pains. Dances such as these are not always refined, but move us as expressions of the courage and the legitimate satisfaction of work accomplished.

More subtle are the dances for two, whose thousand

---

[1] Not that it sublimates it as such. No one is ignorant of the atmosphere of certain dances, but, as we noted above in regard to certain kinds of music, we should remember that the movement which, on the one hand, excites, on the other hand constrains and, moreover, keeps us from dwelling upon it. Even if they are wild and frantic, certain dances have at least had the advantage of wearying the body and weakening the muscles. They leave the agitated people tired. At least they have expended in these dances certain more doubtful intentions. Wherein dancing has filled the function of the lesser evil.

variations are good images and symbols of the complexity of the relationship between man and woman: dances through which are expressed the attraction of desire, separation and misunderstandings, agreement and discord, and the indescribable mixture of delicacy and carnality which is the almost inevitable and universal price of the feelings of a soul united to a body. They are rarely untroubled, but the music imposes figures and attitudes which, even though it may not entirely purify them, at least transfigures their sensuality.

With the *dances savantes*, or rather artistic dances, we enter into a higher realm; the role of the mind appears to have primacy here, for the body is deliberately used in the service of art. Movement has for its mission to serve as a visible and plastic language for an intention other than that of instinct. So the *dances mimées* reproduce scenes that the music inspires: character dances whose figures have a sharply defined significance.

Still higher, we find the pure dance, whose end is not to interpret a determined scene, but to lend a consistency, ephemeral and subtle as itself, to the invisible tracery of music. Here melody is queen and its grace is reproduced in a pure state.

And highest of all is found the religious or sacred dance, arising from a more noble although sometimes less developed type; here the body is associated with the very movement of the soul. Meditative dances, grave dances, dances of homage and supplication, offer to God the best of the human body, its most beautiful soarings, its noblest grace.

All these dances differ in kind and in degree of refinement, but they have this in common, that the center of gravity and point of origin of their movements and figures are situated somewhere higher than the simple faculty of the body to move. That is why the character of the dances which they invent or which they love is a very sure indication of the degree of primitiveness or development of persons and peoples. According to their dispositions, men make the dance a noble or a vulgar thing, something visceral or sublime. Violence or calmness of temperament is not directly responsible for it, but only, and above all, the atmosphere and the rhythm that gratify the heart.

3.

> She rests motionless at the very center of her motion, isolated, isolated, like the very axis of the world.
> —Valéry.

That musical inspiration predominates over instinct and is the very soul of the dance is confirmed by the pure dance. "There all is but order and beauty." Harmony alone, and not the passions, orders all things and reveals the ideal form toward which the dance is striving by its very nature. The whole body is no more than the servant of the rhythm grasped by the mind, and the dancer's efforts are entirely devoted to substituting for his own movements those things that the music proscribes.

In the face of melody, everything else is wiped out, and pure harmony is expressed through the body. And this is precisely the miracle of the dance: it succeeds through its many measures and necessarily successive movements in suggesting and projecting the image of a still purer figure—one that is for the instant unique, at once transient and fixed. Dancing brings into being a real masterpiece by lending to the fleeting moment a consistent action as real and as fleeting as itself.

O flame—living, divine thing! But what is a flame, O my friends, if it is not movement itself, something foolish and joyful and frightening at the same time? Flame is the act of the moment which is between earth and heaven. O my friends, everything that passes from heaviness into subtlety goes through this moment of play and light. And is not flame the unattainable and proud form of the noblest destroyer? Whatever can never happen again must be done as magnificently as it can be done. As the voice chants passionately, so the flame foolishly sings between matter and ether, furiously roars and hurls itself upward.

The dancer smiles at these poetical views. Is he thinking, when he dances, of noble ideas? He believes he obeys nothing but movement, and his conscious effort is entirely ordered to make his body the faultless servant of the music that transports him. Most of the time he is ignorant of the pathetic grandeur of his movements. He cares for nothing but precision and grace.

But are we then forbidden to tell this dancer who torments our senses of the values which his art contains? In his living hymn to movement, he himself sees liberated toward the heights those aspirations imprinted most deeply in his members and muscles. The dance is the most highly developed language of which the total body is capable; it realizes the need of escape from the subjection of weight and necessity, from the fatigue and boredom of everyday life; it also shows a consciousness of the splendor and the fragility of the passing moment. In short, in its deepest roots the dance contains something of our sense of freedom and an awareness of what we may become.

That is why the dance is never merely physical. Whether it is passionate or calm, primitive or developed, its movements belong to an order apart. It arises from a rhythm—we cannot say this too often—different from that which the body performs in response to the world of realities environing it. This is actually the rhythm (perhaps less explicit but authentic) of the vivacity of the soul, at the same time more modulated and more varied than the rhythm that presides over monotonous and slow material changes, over works more ordered and painful. Life itself, in whatever is most fanciful and free, dictates the measure of this rhythm; it is the direct echo of the melody man perceives in himself of his interior song—music. And to this music dancing gives a body.

By its own essence, dancing is the incarnation of beauty and grace—beauty and grace which are, it is true, expressed by the body, but which do not exist solely for the glorification of the body. Not that the dance ever ceases to be physical. But, just as the flame transfigures and exalts the wood on which it feeds and the substance from which it springs, so dancing reclothes the body living it with a movement and a splendor of the face, a grace, suppleness, and completeness and perfection of the limbs and head and shoulders which are no longer seen in themselves: dancing has transformed them into unmistakable symbols of a more subtle, ethereal beauty where the mind, no less than the senses, finds delight.

> I contemplate this woman who is walking and who gives me a feeling of immobility. I am concerned only with the rhythm of her movements.

Let us take care here. Valéry, always a poet, is weighing his words. "Immobile," "rhythm," "movement," reveal the language of the mind and not of the passions. They impose themselves as if they are in the presence of a spectacle whose center is never the human body, even though it is the human body that achieves it.

Dances are rarely so perfectly done that they evoke the flame's pure mounting. Such successes are as rare as masterpieces of poetry. But, rare though they may be, such dances do exist and are the proof of riches and potentialities that the art bears in itself.

The very fact that such dances do exist—have we not seen unforgettable examples?—is enough to prove that dancing is not bad or vulgar in itself, but is capable of enchanting and even uplifting hearts. But simply because it is a human potentiality in which the body must take an active part, it is an art in which full perfection is hard come by. Our weaknesses and passions expose it to many dangers and defects, for an evil genius urges us to go down the lazy slopes of doing the easiest thing, rather than braving the stern demands of pure beauty. But the dance itself is not directly to blame for the inept or perverse use men make of it. Even those who interpret the dance in its lowest sense must first take pains to alter and pervert it, if they are to make it vulgar and ugly. By its very structure and inspiration, a true dance cannot suffer these things. Its very success—and this is its unalterable greatness—is not attained without an interior effort of the heart to impose upon the limbs and upon their motions a little of the real nobility of the purest rhythms inspired by music.

Because it is born of deep things and ascends to the heights, the dance cannot suffer to be treated, either by its admirers or its detractors, as an ordinary pastime or a vulgar manifestation of unleashed passions.

Whether or not men wish it so, the dance requires them to put into it a little of their very heart and soul.

Epilogue

❖

IN DEFENSE OF THE BODY

❖

❖

❖

❖

In Defense of the Body

THE BODY is often treated like an old servant whose faults have been emphasized by too long intimacy.

Many people judge the senses by the moral difficulties they stir up. They speak of their body as "Brother Ass" as if the body is the only thing responsible for all their troubles. Its very presence is an obstacle to them, even a scandal. They reproach it with distracting the mind, absorbing precious energy, and the irreparable loss of time.

Such people would have us think that philosophers are joking when they invite us to discover the advantages in the "substantial union" of the soul and the body. Fellowship with the body, they think, works out to the detriment of the mind. On the religious or moral plane it brings nothing but care and vexation. We are right, they say, to believe it a trial and a trouble. The soul draws no good from its association with the body. A man who wants to save his soul would do well to adopt an extremely prudent and even distrustful attitude toward it, to consider the senses his enemies and the passions as so many snares of the devil.

Such people would say that the only physical activity we

189

can trust is working and fighting for our lives. Necessity confers on productive efforts their claim to legitimacy and even nobility; but there the real usefulness of the body ceases. To expect any spiritual benefit whatever, or any valuable co-operation from the moral viewpoint, is an illusion which experience has shown is vain.

This is what a good many souls of good will and sincerity seem to think: that all desire of attaining the ideal must contain a certain resentment toward physical values. Manicheans as they often unconsciously are, they believe in the total and radical antinomy of matter and mind. Obliged to endure both in juxtaposition, they do not consent to it in the least, in their hearts, and bend every effort to reduce the impressions made by the body upon the mind. As if the mind can be fed on anything but what the body brings! Moral pessimism is always accompanied by masochism; the "spiritualities" inspired by it can always be recognized by the disdainful and implacable character of their asceticism.

1.

At the other extreme from those who are contemptuous of the body we find panegyrists who exalt the carnal life. In all times and under various names—materialists, epicureans, libertines, or atheistic existentialists—they pursue a common work: to promote the cause of the flesh and to exalt the physical senses which alone, they maintain, bring us into tune with what is positive, enjoyable, and concrete. How much weight has this so-called ideal behind which so many men hide their fear of life? Instinct ranges the evidence of its exalting and alluring appeals in favor of this narrow wisdom. Would it not be best to respond to this appeal? The joy of life cannot be restrained; it wants to feel every emotion, and demands the ecstasy to be found at the heart of burning experiences. Lived to the end, passion is itself its own end, they tell us. Whatever the cost, any plunge into the heart of reality, provided it is wholehearted and unreserved, represents one of the high moments of existence.

Let us be frank: reprehensible as it is in many ways, this insolent vitality, anarchistic but sincere, deserves more sympathy than the frozen reserve and the complete, conceited abstinence of so-called "spiritual" people whose absence of temperament assures their virtue. The outrages committed by exuberant natures are more excusable than the hypocritical sublimations of certain moralists whose chief criterion is a respect for appearances.

Now that we have said this much, let us see whether the cause of the flesh as such enthusiasts present it can regain its prestige. Does the flesh gain by being exalted to the detriment of the soul? Much less, really, than the tone of these panegyrists would have us believe. The violence of their words cloaks a highly impoverished conception of the possibilities of the senses.

Those who exclude the mind must fall back on instinct as the cause of our actions. But, taken in the pure state, deprived of contact with any superior principle, instinct is only animal. If we deny that it is permeated by the reason and the will, the immediate consequence is that we must affirm its total subjection to biological animal laws. But these laws create and express the requirements of a dual activity where necessity, from a physical point of view, takes first place: self-preservation and reproduction. Hence the capital place of these two powers in the pleas of the prophets of the flesh.

They elaborate this theme with emphatic commentaries. But the most fertile imagination cannot long conceal their elemental character and relative poverty. Therefore, there arises a temptation to reinforce interest in them by the daring of their words.

This behavior impresses, or seduces, or disturbs (they all amount to the same in the end) only weak minds entangled in the difficulties of neurosis. The barest minimum of good sense is enough to discern the disorder hidden under this fever. Genuine strength does not go to extremes. Only weakness feels a need to show itself daring, to pretend to attain such freedom. In sexual matters, as in any other, noise increases with emptiness.

If they would pay better attention to their senses, sensualists of all kinds would not feel the need of working themselves up to such a pitch of excitement about such elementary functions. Having deliberately limited their horizons and lowered their sights, they are therefore dedicated to monotony. Such boasters are, at best, in the grip of an obsession, and they need moral preaching less than they need medical care.

2.

Who loves well chastises well; and this principle is perfectly correct, for strictness implies respect. We correct only those whose powers we appreciate. Impotency and ineffectiveness are always negligible. The incorrigibility we cannot really suppress deserves the mental suppression that Sartre has marvelously indicated by the word: Neantization.

So the vigilant and strict interest with which the Church surrounds the body denotes the importance she attaches to it. Contrary to what its detractors think, Catholic morality would not be so meticulous and exacting if it did not have a singularly realistic and grand vision of the consequences of the union of mind and flesh. The strict discipline it wishes to instill is a function of the deep-seated optimism it professes. Of all doctrines, Catholicism is certainly the one that expects the most of the human body.

Nevertheless she knows the terrible weakness of the flesh. She knows the part of the passions in sin, the difficulties and the obstacles which, from a spiritual point of view, life in a body creates. But, although many ignorant people reproach her, the Church has always refused to curse the flesh.

The Church has never stooped to pronounce as beyond remedy the misfortunes and wounds of nature. She has always refused to make pact with the facile and fatuous pessimism of those who, even while lamenting it, abandon nature to evil. Catholicism knows the depth and the ravages of evil, but also knows that evil has its limits. Perhaps we have not sufficiently emphasized how much theologians have fought to defend the permanence and vitality of ontological health, in spite of the changes and discomforts resulting from sin. Physical or moral evil cannot alter the essential structure of beings, nor can it prevent their development or diminish their productive possibilities. Catholics analyzing such evil never speak without emphasizing its limits and indicating remedies for it. Their sense of sin does not turn into an obsession, nor their distrust into panic.

Although there are some who accuse Catholic spirituality of disparaging human values and of persecuting the body, the fact is that it is their most generous and faithful advocate. Catholicism has none of the bitterness and scorn to which some of the more arrogant philosophers yield. In a realm where so many others denounce, the Church is obstinate in proclaiming that each person can make a good and pure use of his body and draw magnificent results from it. Far from teaching a solution by evasion, the Church, on the contrary, deliberately consecrates physical activity to the realization of the individual ideal, not only the human, but the religious ideal.

Where does the Church get such confident optimism? If this optimism did not accompany a knowledge of man —a knowledge whose astonishing lucidity and penetration surpass the observation of the keenest moralists—we could call it an illusion. The extraordinary thing about it all is that, while knowing so well what man's world is, Catholicism continues to expect so much of him.

Catholicism makes no mystery of the reason why it dares to hope for so much. Revelation—God's Revelation— makes the Church sure of the value of the potentialities inherent in human nature. The union of the soul with the body was decided upon and brought into being by creative Wisdom, and therefore it has a real and positive utility. That it involves risks need not make us forget its fundamental goodness. Child of God, associated by Him with the destiny of the human soul, the flesh offers resources and advantages that it is necessary for us to know and exploit. Hence the positive character of Catholic morality: the body and the senses are presented as so many aids of the highest faculties of the soul, and not as enemies to be scorned.

It is really strange that this doctrine, admitted on the theoretical plane, meets such tenacious resistance in its concrete application. In everything concerning the body and its senses, negative precepts have taken precedence over positive: pointing out dangers and enumerating precautions have taken precedence over pointing out the normal destiny and virtuous use of these gifts of God. So even in Catholic circles, educators seem careful to set straight the guard rails, to caution and to warn, rather than to direct and encourage.

This timidity and reserve can be explained in part: the world of the flesh is too complex and tormented to allow us to embark on it with naïve confidence. But the body is a capital given us by God so that we may use and develop its resources to the maximum. To do nothing but remain on the defensive is to follow the example of the servant who, when a talent was given to him, wrapped it carefully in a cloth and buried it in the ground instead of using it. This man was cautious to preserve his talent safely, but dreaded the risks its use would involve, and was full of resentment against the Master who had complicated his life with this gift; and Christ said that he was a faithless servant, deserving to be rejected and cursed.

Thus authentic Catholic morality never loses sight of the first lesson of the incarnate Word. In assuming a human body, the Son of God restored its basic value. He has reminded us by His works and His actions of the value of the most humble acts in the eyes of God: in weighing their ordinary actions, in facing their physical duties, men act as servants of God—on condition, of course, that they are in conformity with the Divine Will. The imitation of Jesus Christ, in which true sanctity consists, cannot partake of the abstention and the flight so dear to Platonists, those lovers of the sublime.

Certainly "the infinite distance of the body from the mind symbolizes the still greater infinite distance of minds from the love which is supernatural." But, to be exact, Pascal should have added that this distance does not prevent relationship, fellowship, or even mutual dependence. In the order of nature, the soul can do nothing without the body. And in the supernatural order, grace and charity need both the mind and the body. "The supernatural is itself physical," and here Péguy, a rough poet, surpasses Pascal, a sublime thinker. It goes straight to the heart of the greatest innovation Christianity has given the world. Not only has Christ made His own flesh the instrument and the source of His sanctifying action, but He even expects us to use ours, so that through our bodies He can put grace into our souls.

This gives intolerable scandal to all those for whom union with God can take place only far beyond all finite things, after dizzy ascensions and indescribable nuptial flights. How miserable seem these meetings which take place on the same level as sensory contacts! But here, still dearer, the Church presumes to take literally the words of Christ, as if it would not be enough to take them for pure symbols! It is true that more than any other thing in the world the Church insists on the reality of the Sacraments. She has never hesitated between the fear of enraging those who thirst for pure spirituality and the positive words of Christ. She holds that the economy instituted by Christ is a new proof of the love of Our Lord for His humble creatures.

3.

To this religious realism, Catholicism adds an interest in and a respect for human values which often astonish those who believe it to be obsessed by evil. The Church is following a dual design which extends its spiritual mission of understanding to the defense and restoration of created values.

Throughout history we see her bending over the most diverse works and labors, judging them in the name of morality, but even more so, and above all, admiring them and proclaiming their proper qualities. A priori, all positive and useful things men produce interest the Church.

With pride and care she presents to pessimists and to detractors of human nature the achievements that bear witness to the ontological superiority of good over evil, of life over inertia, of courage over laziness, and of beauty over mediocrity. "Look," she seems to say, "look at the things that, in spite of their feebleness and their faults, their weariness and their cares, their pains and their illnesses, their antagonisms and their hatreds, their misery and their poverty—look at what the sons of God have succeeded in

conceiving and producing. The gifts of God must be efficacious, for often, in spite of the lamentable moral state of
those who possess them, they lead to such beautiful results.
Even if they are sinners, those who so use their innate resources are not entirely bad. Their misery is not complete.
Why should we not admire what they, often at the price of
many struggles and sometimes under frightful conditions,
have drawn out of their skill, their professional conduct,
and their talent? Why be obstinate in seeing only their
sin, whose exact gravity in the sight of God we are never
able to judge? Secular though they may be, human works
have a value which perhaps so-called 'spiritual' people may
look down upon, but which the Artisan of Nazareth judges
well, for He was a craftsman."

Among all the works issuing from the hands of man, the
Church gives choicest attention to works of art. She is as
preoccupied with their meaning as contemporary aesthetics.
She sees them in their total context, and, in this light, considers them one of the highest manifestations of created
power and one of the incontestable proofs of the grandeur
of human activity.[1]

It cannot long be a question of confusing art with the
supreme activities—knowing and loving—whose perfect
acts are accomplished in the center of the heart and soul of
the one who lives them. The work art inspires is external;
and achieving these works requires the use of resources besides those from which knowing and willing proceed. Here

---

[1] The activity of actual labor is well known; so we are insisting here on that of
art, as an illustration of the positive output of the body.

we are dealing with efficacy, with the production of effects. The qualities assuring operative success are different from those that lead to intellectual or religious perfection.

Science, morality, and art constitute three realms that have nothing in common but their human character. Each one has its own laws, style, hazards, and merits; but their development is never synchronized for very long. They do not have the same conditions of success. Except in the moral order, inborn dispositions play a part that no effort can replace. The acquisition of knowledge and the production of truly beautiful works do not depend *directly* upon moral perfection or upon sanctity.

To give art full justice is not easy. Intellectuals and pure scientists believe it a minor activity; and people who wish to be purely spiritual think it a troubling and dangerous activity. Practical minds reproach it with having no practical use. Certainly, art does not pay dividends, in the sense that economists understand it. It possesses neither the utility nor the popular appeal of labor. The transformations it works do not produce utilitarian goods nor industrial resources. The beauty it endeavors to create does not reduce in any great degree the threats to human life.

Is it, for all that, useless? It would be—and the energy expended on it would be entirely wasted—if the vital capital were so stringently budgeted that there could be no question of diverting any energy whatever from the fight for existence. This is not the case. In his very structure, man is greater than is conceded by those who see in him only a purely material being. Through the best part of himself, he escapes from the exclusive servitude of the instinct for self-preservation. He can think of other things besides utilitarian problems; he has enough richness and energies in himself to feel other desires than for bodily security. However great his anguish and his misery, his distress and confusion, he can think and will other things infinitely higher than those concerning his torment. This is called the thirst for the absolute, and this explains his sense of beauty and the importance of what this sense of beauty calls forth. Even if it is useless on a utilitarian plane, the humblest of beautiful works has a mission that is needed infinitely more: it is a reminder of greatness, a witness to inward liberty, a positive proof that, in spite of everything, man can liberate himself from the rule of matter and treat with it as its ruler and its lord.

The artist differs from the workman in that he forces his will upon reality to stamp his imprint on it, while the man who exploits it acts like a beggar. With the worker, craft, knowledge, and technical skill are there to seize upon and hold what material objects are able to give him. But the artist tries to make matter obey him. In the name of his own power and fullness, he draws them out of their own form and confers on them a new value that he himself inspires.

The Church does not minimize the awareness that every artist feels of acting as a creator. We do not expect from the artist the absolute creation of divine action, which draws creation from its own richness, creating by its all-powerful will alone. But the artist who produces a work of art has, by the power of his human personality, forced a change in sensible appearances. This is an activity of a lord and not of a slave, a striking manifestation of the transcendence with which God has endowed His free creatures. It is the triumph of an incarnate mind over matter which so often conditions it, but which it can mark with its own imprint.

The fullness from which such power proceeds is only relative. The intuition of beauty, the decision to produce, the human artistic *fiat*, is never enough, of itself. Creative action can transform something already existing, but it cannot make something absolutely new. In order to become concrete, the most powerful and most original human ideas must borrow their positivity from cold, hard matter. This does not take place without difficulties. More than his genius, the artist must possess and cultivate his native and acquired qualities of execution: talent and craftsmanship. Reality does not allow itself to be easily enslaved.

We must be very ignorant of this labor if we speak of the artist's life as a frivolous existence. The admiration and joy that great works awaken must not make us forget the pains they have cost. "The joy of creating," exaltation and inspiration, the happy exercise of facile gifts, exist for the most part only in books—as also do "the happiness and pride of labor," and "work, holy law of the world," so dear to theorists.

In reality, with rare exceptions, the elaboration of all artistic works is accomplished in fever and hesitation, amid gropings and innumerable false starts, at the price of nameless rages. Imagination does not follow luminous, fervent inspirations; the time of work is particularly crossed with uneasiness, pain, and doubts. What true artist, in spite of his previous successes, is not fearful about undertaking a new work? He knows a great deal less about the secrets of inspiration, the surprises of his metier, and the guarantees of success than theorists and critics do! He enters into his work as an adventure, a plunging into the depths of the unknown. Pretension has less influence in the workshop than in the exposition rooms. The material to be worked demands just as much from the artist in the way of disposition, quality, and authentic effort, as does the conduct of business affairs.

From his encounter with material realities, the artist emerges both exhausted and victorious. Because of such patience and courage, the history of art is like an epic poem, from which shines, moving and triumphant, the fidelity of humans to the demands of beauty. What physical reality has not been conquered? Under the impress of art, heavy stone, cold, rough and mute, is gentled, warmed, and animated. A new form dwells in it and makes us welcome it—a light arch, a gracious column, a statue, laughing or grave, or a proud or poignant inscription awakening the past. Dead wood receives from human hands a life warmer than that of its native forests. Captured by the artist's brush, color is reborn in a light that is sometimes more revealing than that of the sun. Sound, when disciplined by the musician, becomes an echo of interior music. Words, arranged in prose or poetry, contain the marvels of mind and heart. The devouring fire has itself been tamed; its flame, controlled by man, has purified, crystallized, revealed the earth and the sand, the color and the iron, the bronze and the gold. It has united the disparate, suppled the rigid, softened the rough, stabilized the inconstant.

Over each of the indocile or hostile elements, man has

triumphed—in a noble triumph that glorifies its victim. Art makes realities grander than they naturally are. Their material no longer counts for itself: the beauty they contain and express makes this material into a symbol, a message for the mind. "In a work of art," said Rodin,

> what has special importance is what we do not see; that is, what is suggested by the image that we do see. Every work of art is an open window onto the invisible.

By its nature, then, art is never the exaltation of the flesh which so many people fear it is. The Church has understood this so well that instead of remaining aloof from it, she has taken art into partnership. The power art has to evoke effects transforms material realities into signs which, although less precise than words, are just as efficacious. The most uncultured person can understand them. So the Church does not hesitate to ask beauty to put itself at the service of a still higher beauty. Even physical beauty is a child of God. To evoke is not the same as to contain, and to suggest is not to translate or interpret. A symbol is not the same as the thing for which it stands. But is it, then, vain and harmful? Catholicism has never taught that it is. Knowing how little familiar we are with the spiritual, the Church has used any means at hand to give us some instruction about it. She teaches us truth by her doctrine, and suggests harmony and splendor to us by artistic symbols. Their beauty, even though secular, opens a window for us onto higher things and invites those who contemplate them to transcend their material nature. So these works of art are invitation—even bait!—to induce us to think of other things and to think more nobly.

Only those works that are the issue of an authentic technique can be called really beautiful. Beauty has its laws, and the most ardent piety and the best of intentions cannot successfully modify or defy them. So the Church has left artists considerable freedom in their work. The aesthetic quality of the results—upon which is based their power of evoking the spiritual—demands this price. Too, in churches we find works for which the least we can say is that they are not inspired by the canons of taste dear to a languorous sentimentality. Verve and force, daring and fancy are found there as frequently as seriousness. What do such differences matter if they are ennobled by beauty?

But this freedom granted to artists does not prevent the Church from maintaining vigilance. She has the care of souls. So she does not accept anything that could turn men's minds aside from the truth or trouble men's hearts. The freedom she concedes to artists is not a blanket treaty dispensing them from all moral considerations. Let us always notice that the Church's reservations constitute guard rails beyond which art cannot pass, under pain of professional failure (in its own domain). Through her commands in the moral order, Catholicism defends the cause of beauty. The beautiful as such—even secular beauty—has everything to gain by avoiding vulgarity and morbid sensuality. If it becomes gross and bestial, it loses what is best in itself, which is to imprint upon material realities the light and brilliance of the mind. Far from persecuting what is human, religion safeguards its truth and nobility.

The Church has always preferred positive to negative

solutions. So when dealing with art she treats the problem of good from a much loftier viewpoint than many severe moralists are capable of doing. Profound psychologist, the Church knew, well before Freud, that all talent demands its price. The penetration and vigor of intelligence often destroys calm and lays us open to the torments of anguished questions. Talent implies a sensibility that is exquisitely delicate, a nervousness and impressionability that are almost unhealthy. Why should we speak only of these drawbacks? Artists are passionate, vain, quarrelsome! But are they not redeemed by a changeless freshness of outlook, a cordial understanding of people, a childish absence of calculating spirit, an undeniable pride and proven courage? Who can dare to judge them according to the standards applied to sedate people with sober temperaments?

Certainly the Church never calls evil good, nor good evil, but one ought to recognize that she shows a certain indulgence toward these *enfants terribles*. Not that she approves of situations in which vilification and jealousy dominate. She censures the artist even while she is admiring his art, for this is a field where, sooner or later, the best carries all before it, and true talent forces recognition. Are there any other fields like this on earth? Though their methods may be far more reasonable and they seem far more rational, the world of politics or economics, war or industry, have not been able to defend themselves so well against injustice and cruelty. For—let us take careful note of this—unlike great men and heroes of history, whose successes have been obtained at the price of tears and bloodshed, artists have done no harm to anyone. They leave behind them only peaceful and fruitful traces. Of their poor torments and even their tragedies, nothing now remains except their works, which enrich minds and ennoble hearts.

When we have taken everything into account, they remain in the eyes of Catholicism, those among poor sinners who do most honor to the dignity of the body. At least, in their own order, artists have not buried the talents they have received. If nothing else, they help us to understand the value of the nature the Lord has given us. This lesson is not negligible.

To describe some of the resources that man has in his senses is the aim of these pages. Others, probably, would want this explanation to be completed by a study of the moral problems raised by the senses and the conditions of their spiritual use. Let me reply that it is unhealthy to try to say everything at once. There are enough works treating of such things. Perhaps, even, there are so many of them that they tend to substitute questions about the methods of using the senses for the desire to understand well the vital instrument to which they are applied.

And then we speak so often of the pain of man that surely we can, for once, try to write a balance sheet of some of man's joys.

CUM PERMISSU SUPERIORUM

NIHIL OBSTAT: Rt. Rev. Msgr. John F. Reilly, *Censor Deputatus*
IMPRIMATUR: John J. Wright, D.D., *Bishop of Worcester*

Worcester
August 11, 1953